BYZANTINE LEGACY

BY CECIL STEWART

Serbian Legacy

BYZANTINE MADONNA

BYZANTINE LEGACY

by

CECIL STEWART

London

GEORGE ALLEN & UNWIN LTD

FIRST PUBLISHED IN 1947
SECOND IMPRESSION 1959

TO
MARY RIDDLE
WHO STARTED THIS BOOK
BECAME
MARY STEWART
AND COMPLETED IT

PRINTED IN GREAT BRITAIN
BY BRADFORD AND DICKENS
LONDON

Introduction

THIS book is about a journey in south-eastern Europe; in it I have tried to tell of the rise and fall of a great Empire and of the countries and places which once formed a part of it. I have tried to record the almost forgotten heritage while on pilgrimage through Northern Greece to Athos and Constantinople, and through the Peloponnese to Sicily and Italy.

There are many books in which the Byzantine story forms a part, and many which deal fairly exhaustively with particular sections. But it seemed to me that there was so much of genuine interest in the entire field that it really deserved a book to itself. In my attempt to make this work as complete as possible, I have had recourse to various libraries, including that of the British School at Athens, so that my pretence to authority is at times second hand. It is with due deference that acknowledgment is made here and enumerated in the bibliography at the end of this book. I have purposely avoided interrupting the text with annotations—a form of acknowledgment which I consider particularly irritating to the reader, for whom, in any case, such books may not be easily available.

The habit of putting the Byzantine in a rather apologetic paragraph between extensive chapters on the Imperial Roman and the Mediæval Craftsman gives one the quite erroneous impression that Byzantine Art is relatively unimportant; whereas for over ten centuries this Eastern Christian Empire was the guardian of art and civilisation in Europe. Within its extensive boundaries the culture of Greece and Rome prevailed and prospered. Here alone, in the so-called dark ages of civilisation, art and architecture flourished and disseminated an influence which endured long after the greatness and glory had passed away.

INTRODUCTION

Now remain only the memories of that year of travel; recollection can never escape. If passages seem over assertive, the error, I feel, is on the right side. Literature on the Eastern Empire has suffered too long from understatement.

The bulk of the material was written in the form of a journal which I submitted from time to time to the Edinburgh College of Art, the donor of a scholarship which made this journey possible, and for which I shall always be grateful. Much has been corrected and revised, but the original form has, as far as is practicable, been preserved. The photographs and drawings are my own.

NOTE ON THE SECOND IMPRESSION

A number of foolish spelling mistakes have been corrected, but apart from this no change has been made from the original. This book was written over twenty years ago, in the first flush of my enthusiasm, and while some of the purple passages seem in retrospect rather callow, I have not re-written any of the text, for that would mean writing a different book, and, who knows, it might not sell so well.

1958

Contents

		Page
	INTRODUCTION	5
Chapter		
I.	EN ROUTE	11
II.	ATHENS AND ATTICA	18
III.	SALONIKA	47
IV.	MOUNT ATHOS	55
V.	CONSTANTINOPLE	94
VI.	PELOPONNESUS	116
VII.	SOUTHERN ITALY	138
VIII.	NORTHERN ITALY, FRANCE AND HOME	163
	APPENDICES :	
	I. THE HISTORICAL BACKGROUND	186
	II. THE ARCHITECTURAL BACKGROUND	189
	III. THE GEOGRAPHICAL BACKGROUND	193
	BIBLIOGRAPHY	197
	INDEX	199

Illustrations

BYZANTINE MADONNA	*Frontispiece*
	Page
MAP OF THE BYZANTINE EMPIRE	10
KAPNIKAREA, ATHENS	21
SMALL CATHEDRAL, ATHENS	22
S. NICODEMUS, ATHENS	25
KAISARIANI, NEAR ATHENS	28
S. LUKE, STIRIS	31
METEORA	34
OMORPHI ECCLESIA	34
S. NICHOLAS, METEORA	37
MONKS, S. BAARLAM, METEORA	38
METEORA	39
COURTYARD, S. BAARLAM, METEORA	40
AGIOS SOTIROS, ATTICA	41
AGIOS SOTIROS, ATTICA	42
ATHENS	45
HOLY APOSTLES, SALONIKA	48
HOLY APOSTLES, SALONIKA	53
HOLY APOSTLES, SALONIKA	54
THE HOLY MOUNT ATHOS	56
IVERON, MOUNT ATHOS	58
KARYES, MOUNT ATHOS	58
VATOPEDI, ENTRANCE, MOUNT ATHOS	60
VATOPEDI, COURTYARD	61
FRESCOES, ATHOS	63
FATHER GABRIEL	65
MONKS, ATHOS	67
MAP OF MOUNT ATHOS	68
RUSSICO, MOUNT ATHOS	72
GUEST MASTER AND THE AUTHOR, DOCHIARIOU	75
IKON, MOUNT ATHOS	77
IKON, MOUNT ATHOS	78
SIMOPETRA, ATHOS	80
SIMOPETRA, ATHOS	81
SIMOPETRA, ATHOS	82
LAVRA, ATHOS	84
STEPHEN WITH SEMANDRON	86
PHIALE, LAVRA	87
CHURCH INTERIOR, ATHOS	88
FRESCOES, ATHOS	90
REFECTORY, DOCHIARIOU	91
DIONYSIOU, MOUNT ATHOS	92
SANCTA SOPHIA, CONSTANTINOPLE, EXTERIOR	99
SANCTA SOPHIA, CONSTANTINOPLE, INTERIOR	100
S. SAVIOUR (KARIEH DJAMI), CONSTANTINOPLE	103
S. SAVIOUR (KARIEH DJAMI), CONSTANTINOPLE	104
S. THEODOSIA (GUL DJAMI), CONSTANTINOPLE	107

ILLUSTRATIONS

	Page
S. MARY PAMMAKARISTOS, CONSTANTINOPLE	112
CHRIST PANTOCRATOR, CONSTANTINOPLE	113
MOSQUE OF SULTAN AHMET, CONSTANTINOPLE	115
S. DEMETRIUS, MISTRA	119
CHRIST, MISTRA	121
FRESCOES, PANTANASSA, MISTRA	122
PANTANASSA, MISTRA	124
PERIBLEPTOS, MISTRA	125
FRESCOES, CRISSAFA	128
AGIA SARANDA, PELOPONNESUS	129
S. DEMETRIUS, MISTRA	130
THE ROCK OF MONAMVASIA	130
S. SOPHIA, MONAMVASIA	132
S. NICHOLAS, MONAMVASIA	134
S. NICHOLAS, MONAMVASIA	135
ALLIVI, PELOPONNESUS	136
S. MARK, ROSSANO	141
S. GIOVANNI DEGLI EREMETI, PALERMO	143
LA PICCOLA CUBOLA, PALERMO	145
S. MARIA DELLA AMIRAGLIO, PALERMO	147
S. MARIA DELLA AMIRAGLIO, PALERMO	148
S. MARIA DELLA AMIRAGLIO, PALERMO	149
CAPELLA PALATINA, PALERMO	151
MONREALE	152
SS. TRINITA DI DELIA, CASTELVETRANO	154
MOSAICS, NAPLES	159
ARIAN BAPTISTRY, RAVENNA	165
S. APOLLINARE NUOVO, RAVENNA	167
CHAIR OF MAXIMIANUS, RAVENNA	169
S. APOLLINARE IN CLASSE	170
S. VITALE, RAVENNA	171
JUSTINIAN, RAVENNA	173
MOSAICS, S. MARK, VENICE	175
S. MARK, VENICE, EXTERIOR	176
S. MARK, VENICE, PORTICO	177
MARBLE CARVING, TORCELLO	179
CHARTRES	181
CHARTRES	182

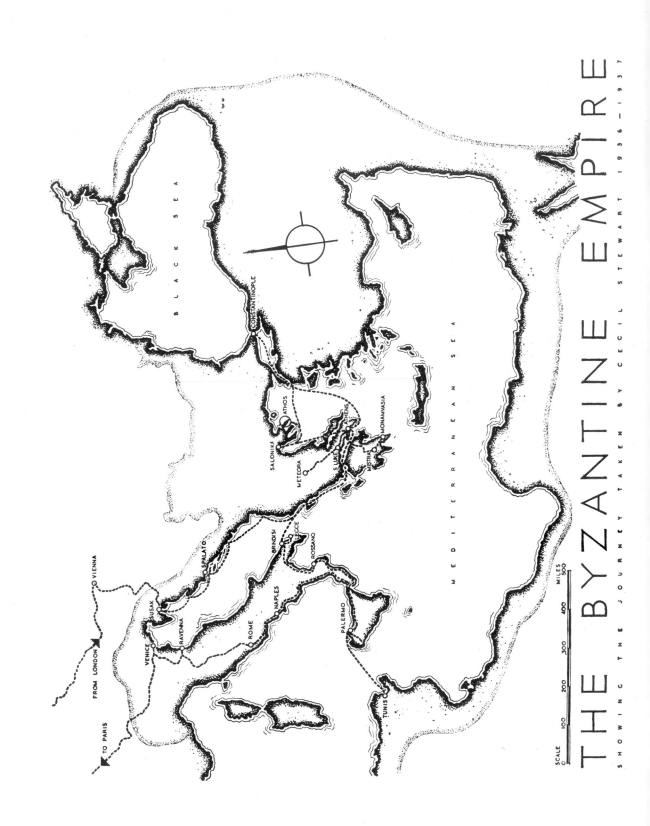

THE BYZANTINE EMPIRE

SHOWING THE JOURNEY TAKEN BY CECIL STEWART 1936–1937

SCALE
0   100   200   300   400   500
MILES

BLACK SEA

MEDITERRANEAN SEA

CONSTANTINOPLE

SALONIKA
ATHOS
METEORA
ATHENS
S. LUKE
MISTRA
MONAMVASIA
GREECE

SPLATO
BRINDISI
ROSSANO

VIENNA
SUSAK
VENICE
RAVENNA
ROME
NAPLES
PALERMO

FROM LONDON

TO PARIS

TUNIS

THE YEAR OF GRACE NINETEEN HUNDRED AND thirty-six was, if you remember, one of travel and record breaking activity. Aeronautical achievements made front page news. Flights to the Cape were accomplished *ad nauseam*. The Atlantic was crossed by the "Queen Mary" in under four days, and shortly after by Jim Mollison in under one. Jean Batten reached Australia in five days. Cambridge won the Boat Race for the thirteenth successive time, and on the night before I left a 731-lb. tunny-fish was cooked whole at the Trocadero. Such, then, was the background which prefaced this journey of mine, and the only record broken was the keeping of a diary for seven whole months ; a feat I never surpassed.

The day of departure was at hand. Innumerable articles, believed indispensable at the time of their accumulation, were jettisoned because the suitcase was a Revelation, not a miracle. Throughout the night of the 18th October, 1936, by a gentleman's agreement, the case lay inviolate at Dover, Ostend and Aix-la-Chapelle, but at Salzburg, on the then Austro-German frontier, chaos ensued, and more by the Grace of God than Man, Vienna was reached. Grace was singularly absent on the part of the Customs officials at Salzburg. Every intimate item was an object of gross suspicion. The Flit spray, on which I placed an inordinate amount of faith (alas, unjustified), particularly outraged their susceptibilities.

VIENNA.

Vienna is the home of Baroque architecture at its best. The local artists broke free from the Italian tradition so that they might evolve an exuberant and fanciful setting for the pomp and circumstance of that remote, but still attractive, epoch, when art for art's sake really did mean something.

To dazzle the spectator with sheer technical ability, along with cheerful and vivacious irresponsibility, was undoubtedly the principal aim of the Baroque. Architecture only paved the way for the architect to drive his superb but sadly overburdened equipage of painter, sculptor, carver, and gilder. There can be no doubt that on many occasions he drove with magnificent, if somewhat careless, abandon. The vogue of the framed picture and the advent of the Gallery exhibition have considerably divorced the painter and the sculptor from the mother art.

Just off the Ringstrasse stand the Karlskirche and the Belvedere Palace, the Lords Spiritual and Temporal of High Baroque. It is obvious at a glance that the Karlskirche was the crowning work of Fischer von Erlach. But as a church, it is really most unusual.

The great patinated copper dome, oval in plan, which surmounts the composition, is Baroque of the Baroque. As Sir Reginald Blomfield has pointed out, one is always in doubt as to whether it looks best end on or sideways. Connected, but at a low level, left and right, are two pavilions with strange gables and even stranger cupolas. In between these pavilions and the centre façade, in a final incredible impertinence, are set Trajan columns, graven spiral-wise with the life of S. Carlo Borromeo and surmounted by a lantern and a copper dome. Only von Erlach could have formulated such a fantastic conglomeration of units, without any one of which the building would be incomplete.

WEST PAVILION
KARLS KIRCHE

VIENNA.

There is a platitude to the effect that one half of the world does not know how the other half lives. That it is so is no fault of the Corporation of Vienna, who periodically expend public money in making the state of their people common knowledge by illustrated publications. The poor in Vienna are very poor indeed. To accommodate the masses of unemployed, the recent Government has been compelled to provide some form of housing till adequate remunerative work can be found.

Rudolph, secretary to the Minister for Housing, had, in that capacity, escorted me over the newest block of flats for the unemployed. There I had met Mrs. Schwartz, a young mother of five children, whose husband each day worked on the new arterial roads outside Vienna for the sum of one shilling per week, given by the Government. So, it seemed, did most of the inhabitants of the block.

The flat was of minimum dimensions and astonishingly clean. Mrs. Schwartz, emburdened by the shyness and curiosity of her children, took pains to show us over. We stayed and chatted, sitting on hard wooden chairs, until we rose to go. Thanking her, I gave each child a shilling, the smallest change I had. They viewed the coins wonderingly, and then with one accord handed them to their mother. She gave a faint gasp as one small hand after another deposited the silver in her palm. She looked at me and stammered things. Her eyes began to look dangerously moist and I hastily patted heads all round and made for the door.

Strangely enough, the poverty of the inhabitants is not apparent, and not until later, when I was sitting in the most expensive bar in Vienna, was the full realisation borne upon me.

" Have a glass of sherry ? " asked Rudolph.

" Thank you."

And he tossed five shillings onto the waiter's tray.

Five shillings, so casually discarded by Rudolph, reminded me of my recent disbursement, and it was then I realised that just such a sum was the total income of the Schwartz household over a period of five weeks.

EN ROUTE.

To me, the joys of travel are very little connected with journeying Wagons-lits. It is merely time spent in getting from one place to another ; a period of stuffy or draughty monotony, relieved at intervals by visits to the Restaurant car, where, under a pink and yellow lampshade, indecipherable menus are followed by peculiar wines and more peculiar food. No, the joys of travel await one at the terminus.

Unique to travel east of Vienna are the uniformed guards along the line, standing to attention as the train passes ; immobile till we are out of view. And at the station, too, they stand stiffly distributed along the platform, giving us a feeling of importance as though travelling in state. Throughout the journey they are never seen standing at ease, and one has the fantastic impression that they are so many toy soldiers from Chauve Souris.

SUSAK.

The interest of Susak lies in its association with that extraordinary mountebank, Gabriele d'Annunzio. There had been considerable controversy at Versailles as to which country the town of Fiume and its attendant suburb, Susak, should be attached. Fiume was then under the control of Maltese and U.S. police. D'Annunzio, poet and soldier, convinced that the district was Italian, made known to President Wilson his feelings, and on the night of the 11-12th September, 1919, with a band of followers, and in defiance of the Italian Government and the whole of Europe, captured the city, proclaiming himself ruler. He grew ambitious and meditated territorial expansion of his puppet state along the Dalmation coast. The Italian Government, however sympathetic they might be and no doubt were, gave him no support. It remained to fix an exact frontier, and by arrangement with the newly formed Jugo-Slav Government and Italy the town was split, the greater half going to Italy and the immediately proximate suburb, Susak, to Jugo-Slavia. D'Annunzio retired to obscurity ; and so it remains.

13

SPALATO.

I took ship down the Dalmatian coast, which, with its great bare mountains of strange and unexpected contours, suggests some primæval unfinished world of wild and desolate grandeur ; and so arrived at Spalato, or Split, as it is now called.

Spalato was a city of transition, both political and architectural. With the decline of Rome, Diocletian elected to build a Palace nearer to the European-Asiatic frontier. From his decision there arose Spalato. This first stage in the eastward trend of the Empire was followed up by Constantine, who chose the more strategically placed Byzantium, later to become Constantinople. The architecture of Spalato, freed from the discipline of Imperial Rome, grew more receptive and absorbed eastern influences, producing a less formal, almost Baroque, Roman. It was, in fact, the first real break with classic purism, opening up possibilities in design then unrealised, but which ultimately led, after a further easternising process, to that perfect combination of East and West which is the Byzantine style.

The Hotel Slavija is situated within the precincts of the Palace of Diocletian. At the entrance is a brass plate inscribed in three languages, one of which seemed familiar :

" RECOMMENDS ITSELE TO THE ESTIMABLE PATRONAGE OF HER GUESTS AS A RESTAURANT AND COFFEE HOUSE WITH FISCH SPECIALITIES "

which seemed inviting, and upstairs in my room I was confronted with :

" ON LEAVE THE HEY TO THE PORTER."

This suggested that greetings should be suspended until the day of departure. These notices might be worked up, I thought, into a very funny paragraph, but reflecting that Mr. Beverley Nichols could probably do it a great deal better and get at least three pages out of it, I made my way to the peristyle of the Palace.

Here, surrounded by the great arched columns which flank the approach to the Mausoleum, is the colossus of Bishop Gregory of Nin. This great bronze statue by Mestrovic appears to be crowded in on every side and one comes upon it suddenly, towering over one with great green flowing robes and spidery fingers, like some fantastic legendary giant. Its magnificence is unquestionable, but how much better it might have appeared set by the water front. There is the danger, of course, that the dramatic value would be too great, and the unfortunate possibility that it might be likened to the Statue of Liberty.*

It is a strange fact, for which I know of no reasonable explanation, that such a gigantic statue should have been erected to a man about whose life so little is known. Endeavours on my part at Spalato to elucidate the mystery of this man resulted in the meagre discovery that his life was devoted to the defence of the Croatians' right to use their own tongue at Mass.

It is a pity that such a work of art should have been erected on so flimsy a pretext. Accepting the dogma that art knows no boundaries, this great work might be a justification in itself. As it is, it has only æsthetic significance, but my firm belief is that art at its best has been limited, if not invariably, at least in a great many cases, by functional

14   *The statue has now been erected outside the walls in front of the Golden Gate.

considerations. Byzantine art, with which we are most concerned, flourished superbly when limited by the rigid code laid down by the ecclesiastical authorities. In the same way, architecture, the mother of the arts, has always been at its finest when, truthfully expressing material and construction, it fulfils the rule of fitness for purpose. This work, a magnificent advertisement of Mestrovic's art, seemingly has no function other than æsthetic, and I cannot believe that æstheticism alone is sufficient to justify such a colossus.

Behind the statue, and approached by steps on either side, lies the Mausoleum, built at the beginning of the fourth century by Diocletian, last of the pagan Emperors of Rome. To construct this building, architects from Greece and Antioch were employed, and here is first made evident that happy combination of East and West which, two centuries later, was to culminate in the perfect flower of Byzantine achievement.

15

The characteristic of Byzantine design is the covering of a square with a dome. The problem is not so easy as it sounds. The Romans had been able, in the Pantheon, to set a dome upon a circular drum, so :

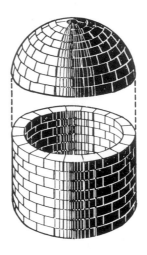

This was comparatively simple. It is much more complex to effect the transition from the square. In Syria, attempts had been made by means of laying slabs across the angles, so resolving the area into an octagon.

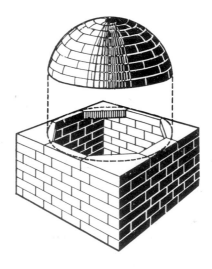

This naturally resulted in exposing unfortunate flat triangles at the corners. But in the Mausoleum at Spalato, another method was adopted, that which is technically known as the squinch. This is a series of small relieving arches springing across each angle to form the octagon on which the dome is built.

16

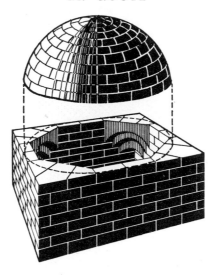

The final and completely perfect form was not achieved until the erection of Sancta Sophia, where the introduction of the pendentive or curved triangle ideally solved the transition from square to circle. This was undoubtedly the great constructive achievement of the Byzantines, and however much one may admire the Mausoleum at Spalato, it is at best no more than an imperfect structural compromise.

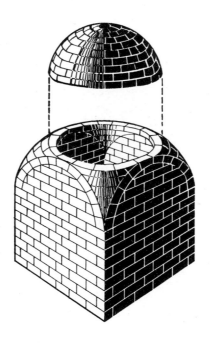

CHAPTER TWO

SURELY NO GROUP OF BUILDINGS IN THE WORLD has been more vividly and ecstatically described than the Acropolis.   Never have sentences been more lavishly filled with superlatives.   Never have ruins occasioned a more profound feeling of despair.   Great as are the remains, how much greater were they before.   The chronicle falters . . . Ichabod . . . the glory has departed.   Nowhere is more apparent the grandeur that was.   The tragedy of the Acropolis is not that it was used as a powder magazine by the Turks and blown asunder by the Venetians, but that a countryman of mine should have been allowed to acquire the greatest treasures, to house them against the grey, sunless walls of the British Museum.   The guide book is pregnant with phrases such as :

> " The sculptures of the east pediment, representing the birth of Athena, an admirable group of sculptures,' were removed by Lord Elgin, 1800-1804. . . ." '

" The fifteen metopes from the south side, and one from the north, are in the British Museum.   There is, however, one in good condition in the south-west angle. . . ."

That he should have left this solitary one was irony indeed.   The sculptures of the Parthenon were designed with care unsurpassed so that they should look just right in their setting of sun and sky.   To transport the beauties of the Parthenon to Bloomsbury was unforgivable.

> " Survey this vacant, violated fane ;
> Recount the relics torn that yet remain. . . .
> Daughter of Jove !   In Britain's injured name,
> A true-born Briton may the deed disclaim.
> Frown not on England : England owns him not ;
> Athena, no !   Thy plunderer was a Scot."   (*Byron*).

Of particular interest in this present study is the fact that the Parthenon, during the reign of the Byzantine Emperor Basil II, commonly known as the " Bulgar Slayer," was converted from a temple to a Christian church.   Basil thought it was a pity that so fine a building should be so bare inside, and decided to celebrate his victory over the Bulgarians by introducing fresco decoration.   Since the building's destruction by the Venetians, however, these decorations became alfresco, so that the evidence to-day is very faint and it is only on the south wall that haloed figures can be defined with any clarity.

ATHENS.

The Hellenic tourist is too easily persuaded that broken colonnades and amputated sculptures constitute the greatness of Greece. This is unfortunate, especially as in Greece alone is preserved to some extent the heritage of an Empire which lasted longer than any European polity before or since. Throughout Greece, and in Athens itself, innumerable Byzantine churches stand to-day much as they were a thousand years ago.

It is true that Athens, which had for so long represented idolatry, became with the advent of Christianity a mere provincial town, and its churches, as a result, cannot compare in size with those of the new capital, Constantinople. They are, in fact, extraordinarily small; precious gems set incongruously amidst the ever changing streets of modern Athens.

It is necessary at this stage to explain that the majority of the churches throughout Greece represent the culminating phase in Byzantine design. I have described how the pendentive is the marked feature of Byzantine building, but in addition it must be appreciated that the internal adornment to some extent dictated the plan and sectional form of the church building. In those days of comparative illiteracy, the church was used as a vehicle for describing the lives of the Orthodox Saints and Martyrs. It became, in fact, a gorgeous picture book in which every available space was covered with fresco or mosaic according to a rigid code set down by the ecclesiastical authorities.

Planned as a cross in a square, Byzantine churches from the eleventh century onwards have the dome raised above the pendentives on a drum. This drum and dome, with its pendentives, cover a square, from which branch four arms in the form of a Greek cross. These arms are vaulted, and carry the thrust exerted by the cupola.

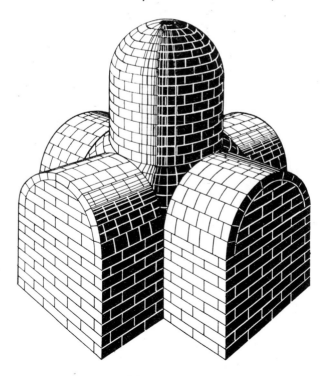

19

There remain, at the angles of the cross, four squares, which are domed or vaulted at a lower level ; thus the whole building forms a square. From the eastern end project three apses, cut off from the main building by the Iconastasis, the centre and largest of the apses housing the altar.

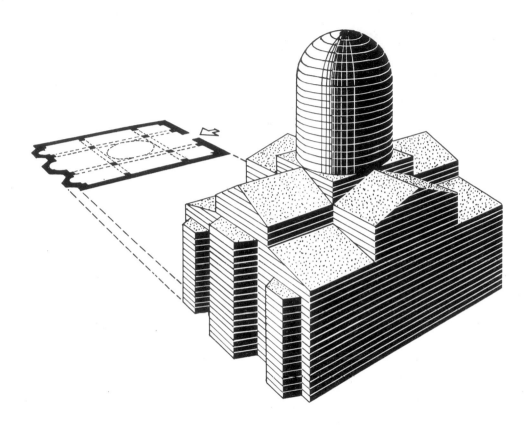

The Church of Kapnikarea, standing in the middle of modern Hermes Street, follows this type. To those unfamiliar with the Orthodox Church, these descriptions may not at first convey the striking characteristic of Byzantine architecture. The English Church is distinguished by its marked vertical lines, its buttresses and its apparent upward thrust. The Orthodox Church, on the other hand, is a building of mass, not lines. The whole building is intrinsically tied together in complete structural unity.

Inside, the contrast is even stronger . . . all is peaceful and shadowless ; the means of support are obscured in an unbegotten, misty haze which wraps like a shroud the mystery of the Orthodox Church. There is present a feeling of uncanny majesty and ageless dignity, which is peculiar when one realises the Lilliputian size of the actual building. The dome, carried on four columns which mark the central square, is scarcely six feet in diameter ; perfect in proportion, encrusted with gold mosaic, it shines from above in a lustrous, unearthly glow.

KAPNIKAPEA, ATHENS   21

SMALL CATHEDRAL, ATHENS

Twenty-seven years after the death of Diocletian, on the 11th May, A.D. 330, the Byzantine Empire was inaugurated by Constantine and was to endure for eleven hundred and twenty-three years and eighteen days, with Constantinople its capital. Stretching from Trebizond to Aquitaine, the Empire flourished, and throughout that time one fact in particular remains . . . a Roman Emperor reigning in autocratic majesty at Constantinople. The constitution and laws were the principal heritage of the Roman Empire ; the throne was elective, the Senate, the army and the people the electors. The Emperor exerted absolute rights. He alone could appoint or dismiss the Ministers, he commanded the Imperial forces and he was the temporal head of the Church. But if he did not give entire satisfaction, the electors could always proclaim a new Emperor. This they not infrequently did. The reigns might be short, indeed they generally were, but they were absolute. Invariably they terminated with assassination, murder or deposition. Starting with Constantine the Great, through a series of Leos and Justins to Michael III, the Drunkard, and Basil I, the Macedonian, the Empire ended abruptly on the 29th May, 1453, with the Mohammedan invasion.

Throughout this epoch the cultural influence of the Greeks was always present, though Athens, the Greek capital city, which had for so long been a stronghold of paganism, had become a mere provincial town of comparative poverty. The glorious temples, in a semi-ruinous state, were converted to Christianity by Imperial command. In and around the city, even the sites of Pagan temples were assimilated into the Christian scheme. Pentelic marble slabs, enriched with antique devices, were used in the construction of new churches. Classic columns, denuded of architrave and cornice, supported the domes. In the Small Cathedral, Antique and Christian slabs are fixed side by side in curious juxtaposition. At a high level the months are represented by carvings of pagan festivals and Zodiac signs. On the wall of the apse a pair of wrestlers are portrayed in perpetual embrace. Prolific egg and dart fragments are interspersed with Christian slabs of crosses surrounded by lions, eagles, dragons and sphinxes, revealing a marked Oriental influence.

Adjoining the Small Cathedral, a monstrous contemporary parody raises unsightly pink and white walls. Known as the Metropolitan Cathedral, it was this day, the 19th November, 1936, a point of pilgrimage from all around. At dawn, a salvo of guns had greeted the approach of the late King Constantine and his wife Sophia, the deceased parents of the present King George, who, after spending their last days in exile, were returning in Royal cortège to Athens. From a simple tomb in Italy they were exhumed and shipped to Greece, there to lie in state upon imperial purple in the Metropolitan Cathedral. An apparently interminable crocodile of school children wended its way along the adjoining streets. Two by two, wearing white shirts, they filed between the watching crowds, shuffled slowly into the Cathedral, passed the beflagged dais on which the coffins rested, and emerged by another door. Meanwhile, the crowd vaguely watched, with that peculiar languid gaze which belies their irascible, curious nature.

ATHENS.

This evening the crowd had thinned, and the Small Cathedral, which had been inaccessible all day, was now open. Sight-seeing, earlier, had been impossible, but now one could look around at leisure. This strange church, dedicated to Panagia Gorgoepikoos, while small outside, is minute inside, accommodating as it does only twenty people. Churches like this were not designed for congregational use so much as for occasional private worship. Here, cut off from the noise of Athens, is peace and quiet. Above, in the dome, a fresco of Christ Pantocrator looks down with terrifying grandeur, the only painting which the church retains from Byzantine times.

The painter in those days followed a formula that has been adhered to throughout the centuries, the only deviations being those of technique and drawing. The primary aim was not decoration but instruction. The painter's duty lay in the expression of a general ideal rather than his own personal emotions. Controlled by these limitations, Byzantine art flourished incredibly. Artists worked in accordance with a simple code, any deviation from which was prohibited. Conventions were used to avoid confusion ; conventions imposed in the manuals of the authorities.

S. THEODORE

ATHENS.

The Church of S. Theodore, by the Garden of Cilanthmon, follows the cross in square plan, and has in addition a bell tower, an unusual element, attached to the northern arm. But interest is centred on an inscription over the entrance door to the effect that the church was repaired in 1049. This church, externally in perfect preservation, was *restored* before our first cathedrals were even thought of. Historically, the Byzantine Empire was at its height long before 1066 and all that. In the remote era of Norseman and Viking, the work of restoration was being carried out on a church as old then as S. Paul's in London is to-day.

ATHENS.

It is necessary, at the risk of tedium, to consider yet one further development of Byzantine architecture. Mention has been made of the squinch, and it may be recalled that this consisted of arches flung across the angles of a square until an octagon or polygon was reached on which the dome might be carried. A later and more subtle development of this is apparent in the Church of S. Nicodemus, where the square is distinguished by twelve piers, one to each corner and two to each side. From this square the octagon is arrived at by large arches rising over the angles and enclosing fan-shaped concavities

S. NICODEMUS, ATHENS

The octagon thus achieved, small pendentives complete the circle on which the dome is carried.

The Church of S. Nicodemus has unfortunately been considerably restored in the last century. Little remains to record ; a frieze of Cuphic lettering adorns the exterior, carried out in brick set in wide margins of mortar.

The use of brick and tile was a legacy from Roman times. In Byzantine building, while its use was primarily constructional, for it made a good joint between uneven masonry and was an easy medium for arch voussoirs, it was used extensively as a means for enriching the exterior. Separating each stone vertically and horizontally from its neighbours, these vivid red lines of tile or brick, set in thick bands of mortar, enhance considerably the external effect.

ATHENS.

The Greeks have only recently been initiated into the questionable joys of hiking. Each week-end they travel in bands across the plains of Attica, carrying knapsacks on their backs. With walking sticks and dark, bronzed faces, they trudge along the Sacred Eleusian Way to Delphi, to Parnassus, and, nearer at hand, to Mount Hymettos. Periodically, at villages, a halt is called, a camera produced and the inevitable group photograph taken.

At my table in a café, a young man was mounting innumerable snapshots with infinite care, each one portraying the characteristic knot of grinning faces. Idly regarding his efforts, my attention was suddenly concentrated by the realisation that the background of these groups was quite frequently a Byzantine church. My interest completely aroused, I addressed him in French, to which he replied in English.

He was interested in photography ? No, not very ! I supposed he was mounting these for someone else ? No, they were his own. He took a lot of photographs for one so indifferent to the craft ? Yes, he did.

This was getting me nowhere.

Perhaps he would join me in a cup of coffee ? Yes, thank you very much. Why did he take so many photographs ? They were records of the Olympian Hiking Club ; everywhere they stopped he took photographs, and when he returned he sold them to his friends.

26

There followed an involved financial monologue, which only went to show that at the end of a good season he was just so much better off than his fellows. But I didn't care much. Perhaps some more coffee? He would be charmed. Was he interested in churches, since he seemed to photograph so many? No, not at all, but one had to have some sort of background and he supposed a church was as good as anything else. I said I was studying Byzantine churches and would like to see his photographs. He shrugged his shoulders and passed the album across, settling back in his seat. Where was this church? And this one? And this? He answered me vaguely at first, only becoming intent when he pointed with a chubby finger and ejaculated " Hèlène," and then sank back.

Later he thought he had better be getting along. But how unsociable of me, I realised. Was he sure he would not have another cup of coffee? And who was Hèlène, anyway? Perhaps she would marry him, one day, and another cup of coffee would be very nice, thank you.

So the cross-examination proceeded, and by the close of the afternoon I had compiled a long list of places, of which the majority were unfortunately completely inaccessible in the time at my disposal, and Leonidas, for that was his name, was replete with about a quart of coffee.

Attica abounds in Byzantine treasures, but in proportion to their distance from classic remains the journey to them becomes increasingly arduous. The country is full of these memorials to a great Empire. Their importance should not be disparaged. That no record has as yet been made is the fault of travel agencies. The day must come when the tourist will no longer be attracted to fragmentary temples. This work of mine can only indicate a possible source of investigation, for there must be the research of years to complete any comprehensive study. Till that day they must remain comparatively unknown.

ATHENS.

The panoramic view from Mount Hymettos is one of the most glorious in the Attic countryside. From the cypress and olive groves which skirt the mountain one glimpses the white sunlit walls of Athens five miles away, the cone of Lycabettus and the Acropolis crowned with the columns of the Parthenon ; and in the distance to the south, the peaks of Pentelicus and Ægeleus and the clear, blue waters of Salamis Bay.

A thousand years ago several monasteries were built here ; to-day deserted, only the abandoned ruins remain, Kaisariani and Asteri being the best preserved. The Church of Kaisariani was founded on the site of a temple dedicated to Aphrodite which was already famed as a place of pilgrimage. Here is a spring which gave assured remedy to barren-ness, as Ovid describes in no uncertain terms. To-day the church's golden walls, laced with red brick and surmounted with dark brown tiles on roof and cupola, present a picture of ineffable charm in the brilliant sunlight.

The building is entered through the Narthex, a porch added at a later date, and it is here that the glorious range of Byzantine colour and fresco is displayed. It has been explained that the artists who created these frescoes were primarily concerned with the

27

28   KAISARIANI, NEAR ATHENS

function. It did not interest them so much how natural or beautiful the portrayal should be ; they were concerned that it should be comprehensible. If it could be beautiful also, well and good ; but first and foremost, function, not comeliness. The Biblical story is told in vivid pictures, never confused by extraneous and naturalistic detail, and through these limitations Byzantine art rose to astonishing grandeur.

In the dome of the church the Christ Pantocrator, head and shoulders encircled in gold, extends His right hand in eternal blessing, surrounded by Angels carrying staves and clad in stiff white, bejewelled in pattern with sapphire and gold and ruby. The pendentives display the Four Evangelists, with pens and manuscripts in hand, seated in front of a rigid architectural background. To the east, in the conch of the apse, the Virgin, in deepest crimson, carries the Infant Jesus, Whose arm is outstretched in benediction. And all around, every available space is filled with episodes in the life of Our Lord and with a strange procession of Saints and Martyrs ; every unit divided from its neighbour by brick-red line and every haloed figure having his particular tale inscribed in coloured letters on the gilded background.

Incredibly beautiful, and of infinite charm, the figures instil one with a strange feeling of mysticism, created no doubt by the peculiar unearthly quality which pervades the whole building, peopled as it is by those unfamiliar denizens of another world.

It is indeed surprising that more is not heard of the beauty of these frescoes—that they should be so little known. For here is an art and architecture which but for the Turkish invasion might have continued to exert an influence throughout the whole of Europe, but which, alas, from that date has faded into comparative obscurity. Yet these churches and frescoes in Greece are alone of their kind. The architecture of Greece in the Middle Ages had developed into a particular style, a style inherited from Sancta Sophia yet clearly distinguished from it, and buildings like Kaisariani are the flower of this achievement.

The connection between the work of these Greek artists and the work of El Greco has already been emphasised by others. His dependence is unquestionable. Architecturally, the only comparisons to be found west of Italy are in the domed churches of Aquitaine and in the sculptured ornament throughout the Romanesque period.

EN ROUTE.

Railway travel in Greece is always something of an adventure. To those uninitiated, like myself, the idea of a lengthy journey on bare, wooden slats does not seem particularly inviting ; and so I suppose it was inevitable that, in a country whose exchange is so favourable, travelling first class seemed a happy possibility. I travelled alone, my seclusion undisturbed, till after the train had shaken past the outskirts of Athens. Then I realised that the carriage was alive with indescribable crawling creatures. Out of every padded seam they crept. For the first half hour a bloody massacre of the parasites occupied my every moment. Still new contingents arrived on the field, in an apparently unending stream. Attempts to stem the tide proved to be without avail, and it was with considerable relief that I felt the train slowly coming to a halt. We were in the middle of the Attic plain ; why the train had stopped here I did not know. My only thought was of changing compartments, and from there I travelled third class. I had wondered at the station why people had stared at me as I sat in solitary state, the only first class passenger. Now I knew.

This halt is the first of many, as this particular line seems to have a single track only, and at intervals a loop where trains can pass. Here we stop and wait until another train draws alongside. And if you imagine that now, after a considerable delay, we shall just puff off, you will be quite wrong. On the contrary, the arrival of the other train proves to be a social occasion. Windows are dropped open and compliments are flung across the intervening space. And although throughout this interlude whistles are periodically blown up and down the line, no one pays the least attention. In fact it is not until our engine driver has said his farewells to his opposite number and strode the length of the train that any apparent decision is made. Then, with a hoot and the clanking of couplings, we are off to the next rendezvous.

From Levadia one takes the local bus to Dhistomu, a journey along the side of Parnassus. From there the trip must be made on foot or on mule; and for a couple of shillings a cadaverous, almost grotesque, creature, with an optimistic guide, is forthcoming to carry me the final distance of about ten kilometres. And so, after a day's journeying, the distance from Athens to the Monastery of Agios Loukas, is accomplished; a span which, to that exasperating bird who invariably flies in straight lines, would involve a flight of only thirty miles. But at last the destination is reached, and only just in time. The gates clang behind us, as the monastery is closed to the world at sunset.

The church buildings are larger than any of their sort I have yet seen, and in the rapidly diminishing light it is only possible to appreciate their bulk. The steady drone of intoning priests, which had cast a mystic atmosphere over our approach, now ceases, and from the door of the larger church of the two there process the monks, headed by their abbot, who comes to greet us. These monks, with long beards, are clad entirely in black. The younger ones, whose hair still retains the colour of youth, have a faintly sinister air, while the older priests, with white, flowing locks, exude a supermundane benevolence. Rather like Father Christmas in mourning.

The abbot speaks first in Greek, and then, to my surprise, he slowly mouths the words: " Where . . . you . . . are . . . from ? "

" From Scotland," I reply, and am forthwith conducted to the guest chamber, to be regaled with a minute glass of ouso, that precious nectar distilled from the skins of grapes, to which is added aniseed, and glyco, a sweet, sticky preserve.

" Edinburgh is very big ? "

" Yes."

" But how big ? Bigger than Athens ? "

" Yes."

They shake their heads knowingly.

" And Lloyd George ? " pipes a young novice, straight from school, who evidently wishes to air his knowledge.

" Very small." And this witless remark produces hilarious mirth from the knowing and enquiring whispers from the others.

S. LUKE, STIRIS

After these pleasantries I enquire if I may see the churches, and learn that they are now closed and that it would be better if I wait till to-morrow. Then the abbot leads me to a balcony overlooking the churches and the hills beyond reddened in the last rays of sunlight ; and he says : " Now rest."

THE MONASTERY OF AGIOS LOUKAS.

Wheler, a travel writer of the seventeenth century, referring to the larger church, wrote : " . . . and truly this is the finest church I saw in all Greece next to Sancta Sophia in Constantinople, notwithstanding it is very old and hath suffered much by earthquakes and time." (It will be realised that in the seventeenth century all Greece was in alien hands and that Constantinople at that time was still considered a part of Greece.)

The monastery takes the form of an open square, in which are placed two churches. The larger is dedicated to S. Luke, and is similar in form to the Church of S. Nicodemus at Athens, having twelve piers to carry the dome. The smaller, that of the Panagia, follows the classic cross in square, and is distinguished by a remarkably beautiful drum of eight sides, pierced with double windows and panelled below with interlacing sculptured slabs, enriched with coloured tesseræ.

The Church of S. Luke is made particularly interesting by its exquisite mosaics, which at present are undergoing minor restoration. In the dim church, the glazed units shine with an extraordinary, dramatic quality. Here is an art for all time, an art whose decorative value is extremely impressive. The walls, covered with innumerable cubes of vivid colour, are like a magnificent mural sampler worked in glass. With intense simplicity and primitive and angular precision, each figure is portrayed, no attempt at realism being made. Symbolically, the characters of the eternal story stand stiffly in almost regal grandeur on a background of golden tesseræ ; each cube laid in rigid pattern till the area is covered and the majestic quality of the whole achieved. Never in life have I seen such supreme craftsmanship, such naive and innocent expression of the greatest story in the world.

Here it is possible, amidst the temporary scaffolding, to see at close hand that art for which Byzantium is justly famous, and from this vantage point to observe the traditional method of fixing. The procedure was something on these lines : first, over the wall surface a coat of plaster was spread, and roughened to take a second coat of finer, slow-setting composition. While this was still soft, the main lines were sketched in sepia with a brush, and then, into the principal outlines of the figures, the mosaic cubes were pressed. These cubes varied in size, averaging about three-eighths of an inch square, though on the hands and face minute fragments not larger than an eighth of an inch were used. Then the larger areas were filled, in cubes of many colours and gradations, and the backgrounds completed in gold.

The church is famed as a place of pilgrimage, and it is here on the 3rd of May that great celebrations take place. Behind a marble slab lie the bones of S. Luke of Stiris, and on that day, and a few days preceding, the slab becomes damp and is covered with moisture which has miraculous powers. In a flask nearby some of this potent liquid is kept, and it was a source of disappointment to the monk who showed me round that no mishap or illness had overtaken me so that he might have the opportunity of proving its efficacy. Here, too, is a fragment of the Holy Cross in an ornate silver casket, which is carried round the fields periodically to bring rain or to stop rain, according to the need. The casket, inlaid with emeralds and sapphires, is unquestionably very old.

The floor of the church, irregularly sunken with ages of settlement, is probably the best preserved example of Opus Alexandrinum in the Byzantine world. Here, in geometric pattern, are displayed Phrygian red, white Vrocoumesian and green Thessalanian marbles, having each minute piece laid according to the predetermined plan. With age, the original colours have matured, and variations from the palest ochre to the deepest purple are apparent, variations which considerably enhance the quality of the rigid patterning.

DAPHNI.

Like the Monastery of S. Luke, the church at Daphni, some six miles from Athens, has also mosaic decoration. But where at S. Luke the mosaic only covered the areas above the springing of the arches, here every available space from dome to skirting is enriched with mosaic and fresco. These two monasteries alone in Attica have mosaiced interiors. Only establishments of considerable wealth could afford this more permanent form of adornment. Painting, compared with it, must be considered inferior as a medium ; the richness of colour and textural quality of mosaic places it in a class by itself. These mosaic squares of glass have a thin layer of colour or gold leaf fused into them, and in places are of extraordinarily minute dimensions.

DAPHNI

The church at Daphni is comparatively well known. Here the tourists, travelling along the Sacred Way towards the meagre remnants of the great temple at Eleusis, call a halt. Here the charabancs stop, and for a period the church is filled, ten minutes later to return to its normal solitude. Only alone can the supreme grandeur of the mosaic in the dome be comprehended. There the Christ Pantocrator gazes down in awful and terrifying majesty. This is not the familiar Lord of loving kindness, but a supreme overlord burdened with all the sins of mankind.

C

33

Above: METEORA
Below: OMORPHI ECCLESIA

Externally, for protection, the church is surrounded by a large battlemented wall, a necessary precaution which unfortunately was insufficient to withstand every piratical invasion. The church itself is built of sandstone, with lines of red tile set between every vertical and horizontal joint. The varied use of these tiles is the principal key to a study of the chronology of Byzantine buildings in Greece. In the earlier stages the simplest, purely constructional use was made of the tiles, as it was only a medium to ensure a level bed for irregular masonry and to facilitate the construction of arches. Later it developed as a highly decorative medium in about the eleventh century, to be followed by a marked reaction and return to simplicity, though at this last period the constructional use was no longer apparent, as carefully squared masonry was then the rule. So the chronological order of the churches is not, as is usual, made apparent by the structural form but by the structure itself. The difference between the rich monastery at Daphni and the small Church of S. Theodore at Athens is one of wealth, not period.

KALABAKA.

This desire of mine to record as far as possible some of the lesser known works of Byzantine architecture leads me, by way of a digression, from Attica to Thessaly, some two hundred miles north-west of Athens. Here stand the Meteora, or Monasteries in the Air. The approach is by railway, and for some miles before the destination is reached the gigantic rocks on which the monasteries are built stand out like some mammoth columned citadel, rising as much as 1,800 feet from the plain. Gradually, as the view extends, new rocks come to view, shaped like sugar loaves or vast stalagmites, rising sheer from the cultivated land, worn into these fantastic shapes in some remote period of denudation.

KALABAKA.

I spent the night at Kalabaka, ancient Æginium, where Julius Cæsar on his last campaign joined forces *en route* for Pharsala. It is strange that neither in his writings, nor, as far as I am aware, in any classic work, has mention been made of the extraordinary geological formation of Meteora.

Once there were thirty monasteries, now there are six. The others, no longer accessible, crumble while the foundations endure, but in these six is to be found the same bountiful hospitality which is characteristic of all monasteries in Greece. After each precarious and nerve-wracking climb, refreshment is forthcoming in the form of coffee and ouso.

Founded by the Emperor Cantacuzene in the fourteenth century, these strange establishments suffered considerably in that turbulent age, so that by the middle of the sixteenth century only half their number remained. During the Turkish dominion, the monasteries retained their independence, and their decline is the result of poverty rather than apathy.

The churches, minute in size, display the characteristic classic form. That of S. Stephen is adorned with frescoes, considerably disfigured by the Turks, and preserves in a silver casket the head of S. Caralampus. The Monastery of S. Baarlam possesses

35

the handsomest of the churches. It was founded on the site of a hermitage inhabited by an æsthete of that name, who has since been canonised by the Orthodox Church. The church has a porch at its entrance, extending the full width and adorned with fresco depicting the Last Trump. Here, in meticulous detail, are shown the torments which await the unbelievers. Impelled from aloft by a saintly throng, these rascals suffer perpetual damnation with an air of smug satisfaction which must madden the self-righteous saints above. These latter personages seem by no means at home in their heavenly dwelling, and give one the uncomfortable impression that they really would be much happier gambolling and capering with the little sinners in the red lake below. However, up there they stay, more for the sake of appearance than anything else, bearded figures, haloed in gold and carrying the usual manuscript scrolls. It is customary, according to the inviolable rule of the Orthodox Church, to portray the Damned outside the main building, as though beyond the pale, while the interior is reserved for the more noble of the Orthodox world.

Journeying back as the sun is setting, the stately rocks, rising perpendicular on either side, cast shadows across each other and fill the chasms between ; while the peaks are tipped with the lingering sunlight, the slopes assume a deep purple hue. Some day, with more time to spare, a study in detail must be made. The poverty-stricken establishments of Meteora may not prevail much longer, and when the last monk leaves the means of access may be lost. About a hundred years ago Robert Curzon, a bibliophile, visited several of the monasteries, and then ingress and egress was obtained by means of a net and winch controlled by the monks above. To-day some could only be reached by the most foolhardy Alpine climbers. It must be assumed that the monks, after achieving their objective on these high places, and having created their own haulage system, made complete their impregnability.

There are only two works extant, as far as I know, in which any considerable description is made of Meteora ; the more important being that of Curzon, who in 1850 described his find of two beautiful manuscripts at Baarlam, which he desired to possess and might have got at the cost of a minor revolution between the rightful owners and his Albanian servants. The other work, by Leake, published some ten years earlier, is more concerned with the picturesqueness of the scene and the financial instability of the monks. So far, I believe, no study from an architectural point of view has been made, although the monasteries of Meteora are commonly acclaimed as being of considerable importance, though secondary to the art of Constantinople.

AGIOS SOTIROS.

A violent thunderstorm delayed for three hours a visit to the small Church of Agios Sotiros. During that period, within sight of the church, a mountain torrent rushed across my track, making further progress, if not impossible, at least horribly precarious. When the stream lessened and I reached the church, I was glad I had decided to wait.

This little, whitewashed church, of eleventh-century Byzantine architecture, stands on rising ground and is marked by four ancient cypress trees, one to each corner. Apart from its beautiful simplicity, the church possesses all the features of its period. The

S. NICHOLAS, METEORA

MONKS, S. BAARLAM, METEORA

METEORA

COURTYARD, S. BAARLAM, METEORA

AGIOS SOTIROS, ATTICA   41

AGIOS SOTIROS, ATTICA

frescoed interior still remains in perfect condition, although the craftsmanship is not so fine as at Kaisariani. An octagonal dome, circular inside, is carried on four debased Ionic columns. This church is little known, perhaps because it has no historical or archæological interest. It is just another Byzantine church, truly delightful and of infinite charm. Surely the expression of an epoch may be as easily apparent in the small and simple things as it is in the great and magnificent.

OMORPHI ECCLESIA.

Different in form, but similar in character, the Omorphi Ecclesia, situated in the barren plain beyond Patine, is intimately surrounded by a richness of cypress and olive trees. The dome and drum follow the accustomed pattern, but are carried on two free-standing piers on the west side, and on two walls, which divide the apsidal end, on the east. Faded frescoes still adorn the walls, and both internally and externally many fragments of Byzantine sculpture can be seen. These sculptured panels, having representations of peacocks and animals, severely formalised in very shallow relief and entwined in a foliaceous pattern, are typical of all Byzantine carving.

It is significant that scarcely any examples are known in the East of three-dimensional Early Christian sculpture. Unquestionably this must have been to some considerable extent the result of the revulsion from Paganism, with its naturalised Greek and Roman sculpture. The Hebrew religion, which with its idea of a future life and of an unknown God, prohibited the use of images, had much influence on the Early Christians, who must have felt a similar repulsion to figure representation. The Oriental mind, too, saw things flat rather than sculpturally, shading being the only indication of a third dimension. The human figure is hardly ever represented in Byzantine sculpture, only symbolic representation being permitted.

It may be remembered by devotees of John Ruskin, how he describes with his own peculiar vividness a simple rectangular panel on the walls of S. Mark's at Venice, having engraved in bas relief twelve sheep, six on each side of a throne. On the throne is set a cross and over this, within a circle, a gambolling lamb. Over the sheep is incised in Greek " The Holy Apostles," and over the gambolling creature, " The Lamb." So, in that vigorous little panel is shown in brief a typical example of the symbolic personification which permeates Byzantine sculpture.

The Omorphi Ecclesia still retains the original belfry tower, though its precarious condition has necessitated the removal of the bell, which now hangs picturesquely on a pine tree alongside the church. It is difficult to appreciate what precisely the function of this belfry can have been, for apart from the immediate proximity of one farmhouse, no other sign of habitation can be seen for miles around.

ATHENS.

The Byzantine Museum in Athens is a converted villa, arranged with taste to display an unequalled collection of Byzantine treasures. Rooms are reconstructed in the form of small chapels, so that sculpture and painting can be seen in correct disposition. In addition, several rooms are set apart for the exhibition of ikons, arranged primarily according to subject-matter and country, not chronologically.

The painting of ikons is believed to have originated in Egypt, where portraits of the dead were laid beneath the mummy bands. Like the Byzantine ikons, these portraits were painted on wood, and also display a marked technical resemblance. In early Constantinople, ikons were painted which had miraculous powers. There followed a period of vicissitude in which these powers were discredited and the painting expelled from the churches and destroyed. The Empress Theodora, a firm believer in the paintings, introduced, in defiance of the Ikonoclasts, ikon-toys, smaller paintings from three to four inches wide, which could be carried on the person and worshipped in secret. However, with the reign of Irene, the Ikonodules gained their first victory, and towards the close of the Byzantine era these paintings developed considerably in size and subject-matter. Where originally only single figures were represented, later whole scenes and groups were portrayed. In addition, they were adorned with gold and silver, till in many cases only the faces and hands appeared of the original painting.

Mention has been made of how the frescoes which adorn the churches followed carefully the prescribed ruling of the authorities. So it was with ikon painting. In the Byzantine Museum can be seen ikons, produced in different countries and in different centuries, which appear identical in practically every respect. It is a highly stylised painting in which features are expressed in chocolate colour, with vivid high lights picked out in precise lines of white ; Nature appears in the form of sienna-coloured hills, and trees which are like veridian lollipops on abbreviated stems. The ikon was often the work of more than one : a pupil might gild the background and paint the draperies, but the features and hands were invariably the work of the master craftsman.

ATHENS.

In conclusion of this Attic episode, and so that it might be given some semblance of completion, mention must be made of one or two churches which, though having no especial interest, are typical of the Byzantine epoch. The Church of The Asomatoi, The Angels, or literally, " Bodiless Ones," and the Church of The Holy Apostles, both in Athens, follow the cross in square plan, but have suffered much from alteration in more recent times.

Miles off any beaten track, on the south side of Mount Pentelicon, stand the remains of a monastery called Daou-Mendeli. To-day, in front of the fragmentary ikonastasis, lamps still burn. The church, like many others, is preserved by the peasants as a sort of wayside shrine, although in many cases, as at Daou-Mendeli, the way is somewhat obscure. This church has been one of the largest in Attica and has extensive gallery accommodation which indicates that, like the Monastery of S. Luke, it must have been at one time a place of pilgrimage.

The plan is peculiar to this district, following the Eastern Orthodox type. According to tradition, it was built under the direction of an Armenian monk, which seems a reasonable explanation of its eastern form. The church is built as an octagon, with apses on each side, having behind the ikonastasis a tri-apsidal end surmounted by a semi-dome. It suffered considerably from attacks by pirates from Regina in the fifteenth century,

ATHENS

who massacred the monks and pillaged the church ; from that date the monastery, as such, has ceased to exist.

I had thought it possible, at the outset, to make a fairly complete study of all the Attic churches, but the ultimate realisation of their number has made this impossible. An effort has been made, however, to discriminate as far as possible, so that this study should appear at least reasonably representative.

Greece is a country where the dignity and beauty of ancient things linger long. There alone the great Byzantine Empire lives and endures ; there the Greeks maintain the glorious heritage with the same faiths and customs as their forefathers. Perched high on barren hilltops, and secluded in fertile valleys, these little domed churches are the true and living heritage of Ancient Greece.

CHAPTER THREE

THE JOURNEY FROM ATHENS TO SALONIKA MAY take anything up to thirty-six hours by rail, a distance which can be covered in two hours by airplane. Personally, the idea of air travel still instils the feeling of adventure, a feeling no doubt inspired on this particular day by an exceedingly early start by charabanc, past sleep-ridden houses into fields entwined in writhing mist, illuminated on arrival at the airport by the red glow of dawn.

The engines roar louder and louder, and suddenly the tin shacks of Customs Houses recede and waltz slowly round. The unsteady craft bounces on a floor of white clouds which, after a time, dissolve to disclose the outline of Eubœia. On previous flights I have been disappointed because the area below me did not look, as I had expected it to look, like a map. This time, with the distant horizon enshrouded in flying mist, the likeness of the unobscured area to the map is exceedingly fine, so much so that one almost expects to see the names of places graven in letters of inky blackness on the scene below.

SALONIKA.

Salonika owes much of its interest to the picturesqueness of its inhabitants, peopled as it is in a large proportion by the descendants of those Jewish families expelled from Spain by Ferdinand and Isabella centuries ago. They still wear a similar attire to that worn by their forefathers, and to this day speak the same Castillian tongue. That they should even yet use the language of five hundred years ago is surprising indeed ; but even more so is the fact that these Jews, contrary to their race's normal acceptance of the conditions of the country they inhabit, have so detached themselves from the life of the native population that, with constant inter-marriage, they have produced a particularly marked physical type. They throng the Petticoat Lanes of Salonika, wearing, with singular pride, tall, black hats, trimmed with red fox fur. The trimming is a relic of a mediæval decree which compelled them to wear this symbol of duplicity and cunning to distinguish them from Christians.

Salonika, celebrated by the visit of S. Paul, was an early stronghold of Christianity and one of the last to fall into the hands of the Turks. Situated on the main trade route between East and West, it was a city of considerable importance, and here churches were built which, if they do not surpass, at least equal the buildings of Constantinople, with the exception, of course, of Sancta Sophia. The design of that building, too, is now generally accepted as being derived from a church of the same name at Salonika. This church, considerably smaller in size, though large by Greek standards, was built some hundred years before. Rivoira, an Italian, whose patriotic impulse led him by an exceedingly tortuous route to claim this building as a most important link in a chain

47

HOLY APOSTLES, SALONIKA

connecting the Roman Basilica with the Byzantine constructional system, has now been entirely refuted, the accepted theory now being that the real origin was not Roman but a happy combination of Greek and Oriental inspiration.

Entering the Salonikan church by a striped Turkish porch into the great galleried nave, one begins to appreciate how superb the temple must have been—and still is, for that matter. The semi-spherical dome, forty-five feet wide, carried directly on pendentives, is the earliest known example in the Byzantine world. (The later development, in which the dome surmounts a drum which is carried on pendentives, we have already seen. The simpler and earlier form, which is typified in Sancta Sophia and in the smaller parent church at Salonika, is undoubtedly the most æsthetically perfect constructional shape ever achieved in domical construction.) Over the area of the dome, in mosaic, the head and shoulders of Christ are depicted within a medallion, carried in a Heaven of gold by two Angels and surrounded by the radiating figures of the Twelve Apostles. This mosaic, itself superb, is surpassed in beauty by the Virgin, robed in mahogany brown and seated alone on a field of gold in the apse. This noble figure, set up by Bishop Theophilus somewhere between the years 785-797, supersedes an earlier mosaic of the Ikonoclastic period, which took the form of a simple Greek cross, still decipherable beneath the superimposed layer.

SALONIKA.

During the War of 1914-1918, Salonika suffered considerably and much of the city was destroyed. The greatest losses, however, were incurred in the great fire of 1917, when more than 120,000 were rendered homeless. During that calamitous winter night, when the fire was at its height, the entire Christian population prayed to S. Demetrius, the Patron Saint of the city, that the flames might be abated. But the fire progressed to the very walls of the Patron's church, while the crowd, aware that the edifice had miraculously remained unscathed during recent bombardments, firmly believed that S. Demetrius himself would intervene at this, the eleventh hour. The wooden roof of the church, however, caught alight, without any effort having been made to control the flames, and finally crashed into the heart of the church, where it blazed so fiercely that the marble panelling, and even the monolithic columns which carry the arcade of the church, were shattered.

To-day, ruthless steps are being taken towards restoration. On the broken floor, in orderly rows, lie fresh, gleaming white marble drums, which will replace the beautiful, though shattered, olive green ophite columns. New walls are towering up of bright red brick and white cement, to carry a new wooden roof. It only requires a stupendous poster to be plastered on these walls, announcing the re-opening of this super production, to complete the ghastly picture.

Inside, the damage still remains to be done, and here and there along the galleried nave are column capitals of great beauty of design and exquisite delicacy of execution. It is in the design and workmanship of these capitals that the Byzantine sculptors excelled.

It will be appreciated that the first and most important requirement of all capitals is to provide a suitable seating for the wall or arch which the shaft has to carry. The

D

49

easiest way would be simply to lay a square block of stone or marble on the shaft, so :

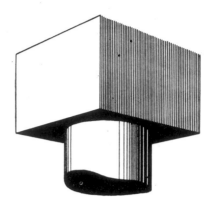

This is, at best, a savage and clumsy answer, and it will be seen that we have arrived at our old problem of uniting the square and the circle. The natural proceeding, then, will be to splay the sides of the cube and cut off the four corners, arriving at this solution :

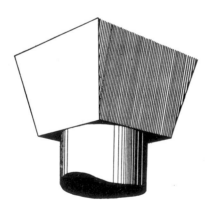
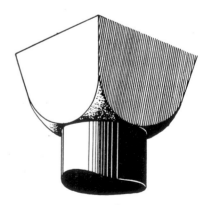

This the sculptor enriched with intertwining and interlacing acanthus leaves, deeply undercutting all round, till the finished capitals appeared to be of such delicacy, like open basketwork, that it was felt necessary to superimpose a second member, to relieve it, in effect, from the weight of walling above. This second member, a happy modification of the abacus and entablature of classic orders, is known as the dosseret block, or cushion cap.

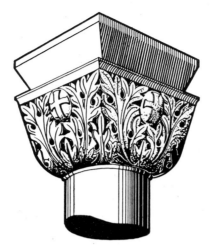

There are, of course, many variations and distinct types, but in general principle the united form of capital and dosseret may be considered typical.

The Church of S. Demetrius, built in the fifth and restored in the seventh century contains many examples of this achievement of Byzantine art, and was also famed for its mosaics. These, discovered as recently as 1907, after being hidden for centuries, were brought to light, to remain for the world's appreciation for only one decade. Of the few fragments left after the fire, one, an eighth-century creation, is of S. Demetrius himself, standing between the original founder of the church and the Prefect Leontius, the restorer. These figures, standing full length, are of incomparable subtlety of design and colour; with a careful interplay of cubes, large and small, the chromatic scale on the face and hands varies from coral pink in the high light to deep jade and lapis lazuli in the shade.

SALONIKA.

The earliest church in Salonika is that of S. George, built by the Emperor Galerius as a Pantheon. Its chief constructional interest lies in the fact that it typifies the Roman structural system. It will be recalled that the simplest form on which a dome can rest is a cylinder, and this example shows such an arrangement with a dome eighty feet in diameter, having walls twenty feet thick to carry its thrust.

Here the sound of one's footsteps, magnified a thousand times, echoes louder and louder with terrifying reverberation as one approaches the centre. The temple, dedicated successively to Roman Paganism, Christianity and Mohammedanism, is now an almost empty shell. In the great dome, once completely adorned with fifth-century mosaic, only the lowest tier remains, that depicting Eastern martyred saints in front of formalised architectural composition. These decorations are lent a peculiar vividness and intensity by the emptiness of the whitewashed walls.

The mosaics in the Christian churches were surprisingly undamaged by the Mohammedans, although most of the Christian temples were converted into mosques. A covering of whitewash was often resorted to if the Christian character was too pronounced. In some cases, however, where fresco was used, the Turks seemed to take a particular delight in attacking with a pick the eyes and other features of the Saints. When one realises the pronounced views of the Mohammedans on figure representation of any sort, this seems to show remarkable tolerance. By way of a contrast, one cannot help noticing the extreme attitude of the present inhabitants of Salonika towards the remains of Turkish dominion, which allows the Mohammedan mosques to be destroyed; buildings which, following the Byzantine tradition in construction and design, provide a particularly interesting corollary. A great measure of the beauty and attraction of Salonika to-day lies in the stately minarets, tall and delicately proportioned, which pierce the horizontal mass of houses like slender ivory fingers. Yet there is even a scheme afoot to destroy these elegant reminders of Mohammedanism. Salonika aspires to Western culture, and their absence from the great Western capitals seems to provide sufficient justification for their destruction.

While the Salonikans destroy all that remains of Mohammedanism, they do at least endeavour to restore the Christian monuments. True, in the case of S. Demetrius it is with apparently misdirected zeal, but in the Church of the Holy Apostles their efforts are to much better effect. This latter church, a gem of fourteenth-century Byzantine architecture, is situated in a square surrounded by cypress and fig trees and stands some five feet below the present pavement. During the Mohammedan regime, the Turks had built up against its walls those innumerable parasitic dwellings which appear to be the inevitable adjunct to all the lesser Turkish mosques. These have now been cleared away, and the exterior is displayed in full glory. While the Athenian churches achieved their effect with a combination of brick and marble, this church is constructed of brick alone; bricks seldom exceeding one and a half inches in thickness, arranged in a multiplicity of decorative pattern, which varies in colour from deepest ochre to the richest sienna.

The frescoed interior has suffered considerably from the assaults, by pick, of the Turks. The effect caused by a thousand white pock marks is that of a violent snowstorm, through which the numerous Saints and Apostles are passing, a storm in which the snowflakes, arrested, never come to earth.

It is difficult to write of these hundred little characteristics which mark the personality of one Byzantine church from another. Differences of setting are perhaps the greatest. Three other churches in Salonika suffer from violent snowstorms in their midst. The most marked distinction of the churches here of the fourteenth century is a profusion of domes. In this late period of development it became customary to surmount the four squares which fill the angles of the cross with drums and domes, smaller editions of the central structure. These external growths, so happily inaugurated here, were finally to develop, in Russia, into that madly exotic exuberance of wild improbabilities which culminated Byzantine achievement in the East.

HOLY APOSTLES, SALONIKA

HOLY APOSTLES, SALONIKA

CHAPTER FOUR

WEATHER PERMITTING, A SMALL SHIP MAKES THE voyage from Salonika to Athos once a fortnight. I left on a calm sea at dusk. As the sun set behind Olympus, giving precedence to the moon, the murmur of Salonika grew dim and the white tower, mediæval guardian of the city, faded into a misty haze.

The evening was cold, and a chill wind lapped up the waves against the sides of the vessel as she bore us into the night. On board, the strange atmosphere of monasticism made itself apparent by the preponderance of monks dressed all in black, with tall, chimneypot hats.

There was present that feeling of tense excitement occasioned by the realisation that this ship was carrying me back across ten centuries. For Athos, last remaining strong-hold of Byzantine civilisation, is known to preserve to this day the identical way of living which was originated with the founders of the monastic settlements. There, it is said—according to the Orthodox Church—no woman has set foot since the Virgin Mary in person gave her approval to the Mount as a dwelling place for the ascetic.

As we rounded the southernmost point of Pallene peninsula, the thin wail of a creature in distress at my feet attracted my attention. It was a cat, dark and sinister. I bent down to caress it, and a young novice came out of the darkness and hastily retrieved it.

" We are taking him to Athos," he said, " we have so many rats."

" She seems rather frightened," I remarked.

" *Him*," emphasised the monk, faintly shocked, as he turned away bearing his small burden.

Then I remembered that all female creatures were barred from the Sacred Mountain. Poor, tragic creature, so naturally amorous, doomed to celibacy.

In the cold grey light of dawn there appeared from the sea the cone of Athos, shrouded in mist. The Mountain, six thousand feet high, terminates a narrow finger of land which stretches, in company with two others, from the northern shores of the Ægean. Here about six thousand monks live, worship and die. As the coastline cleared, it was possible to distinguish here and there several of the monasteries, gleaming white against the cold, blue shadow of the Mountain. The rhythmic drumming of the ship softened, and finally stopped ; and anchor was cast at the port of Daphni. From the shore, two small rowing boats approached the now stationary vessel, and in the company of my friend with the tom-cat and some other monks, I was rowed to land. In the neighbouring boat, a Greek police officer examined my passport, and, my sex being apparently unquestionable, I was allowed to land.

THE HOLY MOUNT ATHOS

The port of Daphni has little of interest. A small inn is inhabited by a few lay work-men, and provides meagre sustenance for the occasional visitor. Nearby, at the policeman's house, my passport is duly stamped and it only remains for me to travel to Karyes, where I must present my letter of introduction, to receive others which will admit me to the hospitality of all the monasteries of Athos. Outside, a mule, in the charge of a ragged Greek whose feet are shod in several layers of bandage, awaits my pleasure ; and upon financial agreement, if such unhappy compromises can so be called, being reached, I proceed up towards the narrow ridge which runs the full length of the peninsula.

Any considerable description of the Athonite scene is scarcely within the scope of this book, but some brief mention must be made of the extraordinary beauty which pervades the entire Mountain. The white and gold weathered marble peak, and the deep sunless ravines, and the occasional patchwork of plantation which surrounds each monastery, and the olive groves and vineyards, and the gigantic trees at the base of the Mountain, all play their part in creating a scene of fantastic beauty.

Reaching the ridge, the dense cloud which had overshadowed my approach turned out to be a thick and penetrating mist, which later, in Karyes, resolved itself into a steady rain. The short journey from the summit to Karyes was exceedingly steep and tortuous over the white marble cobblestones, which seem to have a rather less functional purpose than æsthetic. It is strange that the mule, known to be so sure footed, should instil in its rider such a feeling of insecurity. With a rolling gait, it seems likely to precipitate one at every downward step.

KARYES.

Having deposited my belongings at the Coffee-Ale-Eating-House-And-Hotel-of-Sleep, as the inn is pleased to call itself, I set out for the Civil Governor, there to present my letter of introduction, only to be informed that I should have to return later in the afternoon. This I realised, to my annoyance, would entail my remaining in Karyes overnight, as Vatopedi, the first monastery I wished to visit, was too far distant.

Walking through the vine-hung thoroughfares of Karyes, the peculiarity of the metropolis of Athos is not at first apparent. For Karyes is the only town in the world without a single woman. For over a thousand years the masculine seclusion has been undisturbed. Here no children play, or women gossip. A solemn calm is preserved, almost oppressive in its stillness. A black-robed monk leads a mule along the twisting lane. To ride would show lack of respect. Only on foot can one pass the Church of the Protaton, supposedly built by Constantine, which houses a sacred ikon of Christ, reputed to have cried out, with a loud voice, commanding the officiating clergy to ac-celerate the reading of the Liturgy so that they could administer the Sacrament to a failing monk. Three times the ikon spoke urging haste, and on the last occasion the priest obeyed. Later the ikon became known as Antiphonitis, or " He who speaks on behalf of a man."

At four o'clock I proceed to the Civil Governor, where my letter from the Greek Foreign Office is accepted and in return another is given, which I must exchange yet once more, this time at the Holy Synod. Here the welcome is kindlier, the hospitality more pronounced. Attired in the old national dress of white tights, pleated kilt, em-broidered jacket and a scarlet hat enhanced with the silver eagles of Imperial Byzantium,

57

Above: IVERON, MOUNT ATHOS
Below: KARYES, MOUNT ATHOS

the Synod guard gives me a welcome. In a long, rectangular room, regaled with the ubiquitous glyco, I wait for the precious document that will make this journey possible. Sealed with the Common Seal, it recommends my Learned Excellency to all the Holy Monasteries, and asks that they will receive me with a good heart and with due kindliness and esteem . . . and they remain, Your Brethren in Christ, the Presidents of the Sacred Community of the Holy Mountain, Athos.

This Holy Community is a representative body of twenty members, elected annually by each monastery, which in addition provides a separate residence at Karyes for its member. The primary function of this Community is to enforce the preservation of the traditions of the Mountain, to maintain peace and order, and to settle all disputes of religious and material nature which may affect the lives of its inhabitants.

Historically, little is known of this body before the ninth century. The first documentary evidence exists in the form of a Chrysobul granted by the Emperor Basil, declaring the independence of the Mountain in the year 875. This independence was re-established by the Emperor Leo the Wise, and a " Residence of the Elders " was founded at Karyes. In the thirteenth century the fourth Crusade disturbed the equanimity of the Mountain. Ostensibly marching to destroy the infidels, the plundering horde attacked and captured Constantinople, the fountain-head of the Orthodox Christian Church. Athos was placed under the rule of the Bishop of Sebaste, stationed at Salonika. He, in company with the Western barons, started an era of systematic plunder. In 1430 the Byzantine Empire, considerably weakened, was gradually crumbling. Salonika fell to the Mohammedan invasion, and Athos submitted to Sultan Murad II. Throughout the Turkish reign, the traditions of the monks were surprisingly undisturbed. However, in 1912 the Mountain was freed from Turkish dominion, and in 1923, by the Treaty of Lausanne, the Athonite community was placed under the sovereignty of Greece, that country guaranteeing the rights and privileges of all the monks and the autonomous power of the Holy Community.

VATOPEDI.

I awake to the shouts of a waiting muleteer. Breakfast is frugal, and within half an hour we are plodding along the cobbled track to Vatopedi. Travelling in a northerly direction towards the coast, the journey is made in a few hours. I dismount some distance away, at the command of the muleteer, and with due humility proceed to the porter's lodge, where, having shown my letter of introduction, I am led to the guest chamber, there to be refreshed, by Eastern custom, with a tray containing coffee, liqueur, cold water and Turkish Delight.

From the guest chamber, the disposition of the monastic buildings is manifest. An immense, irregular triangle of multi-storied building surrounds a paved courtyard, in which stand two isolated churches. The painted and weathered walls are like some vast scheme of Picasso-esque decoration ; a plethora of colour encompasses the courtyard. The churches are garnets encircled with a patchwork of chalky blue, pink, white and gold. Externally, the colour is not apparent. Rather it is a veritable walled town like a mediæval fortress, without windows in the lower floor, relieved above by projecting wooden balconies, after the Turkish manner. At one corner a great tower protects

VATOPEDI, ENTRANCE, MOUNT ATHOS

VATOPEDI, COURTYARD

the approach, and from here, no doubt, the traditional boiling oil was poured as protection from piratical raids.

At three o'clock I was aware of considerable activity in the courtyard below, and my meditations were disturbed by the entrance of a monk, fat and jovial, from whose lips there issued a stream of passionate exhortation.

"Prodhoo ! Prodhoo ! " He finally exclaimed.

Up till now any considerable understanding of Greek had been unnecessary. It had been possible, with a knowledge of the alphabet and a fair smattering of French, to manage tolerably well.

"Prodhoo ! Prodhoo ! " He repeated.

This was absurd, and there was obviously nothing I could do but obtain the services of a linguist. Eventually the monk rolled out, happy and smiling, to return, by some strange fate, with Basil, a young chemist from Salonika, spending a vacation on the Mountain. Basil spoke French, and conveyed to me that a service was beginning in the large church and that we should attend.

There for an hour I stood, listening to the strange Balcan service, supported on the crutch-like arms of the pews and gazing at the frescoes, the most exquisite I have yet seen. It is extraordinarily difficult to describe, to those unfamiliar with Orthodox painting, the rigid symbolism, complete mastery of composition and brilliance of colour which characterise the paintings on the Mountain. Severely formal and fantastically bearded, the Fathers of the Church line the walls, each carrying in manuscript his particular lesson. The lines of their draperies, stiff like boards, and the strange elongation of the figures, lend a majesty and dignity to the patriarchal expression of their haloed heads. Meticulously painted in shades of sombre brown, their faces express an almost unworldly austerity and are defined with surprising clearness, considering their undoubted antiquity.

The service over, we proceed through the ikonastasis, a beautiful piece of work in wood, minutely carved and gilded, to the Sanctuary, where from a cupboard various relics are produced by the Priest and Keeper of the Treasures. Every monastery possesses its relics, which are not only venerated but feared. To them the monks pray, and that they possess miraculous powers is never in doubt. The rather sordid remains are enhanced by a luxurious casing of silver and gold, which is studded with emeralds and rubies of terrific size. The priest lifts them tenderly and places them on a bench, previously draped. After kissing each one he indicates that we should follow suit. Here are the skull of Gregory the Theologian, the Virgin's Girdle, the foot of the Martyr Theodore, and a portion of the Holy Rood. Unaccustomed as I am to the kissing of bones, no matter how chastely encased, I hesitate. The priest, however, insists, assuring me at the same time, through Basil, that they will confer grace upon me. The Virgin's Girdle, he emphasises, possesses particular powers in warding off the plague, and has been transported many times to the Near East to give effect to its miraculous potency. This, by the way, at considerable financial gain to the monastery.

This form of inoculation is strangely comforting to the monks, especially as facilities for medical attention are practically nil.

FRESCOES, ATHOS
63

We were then led to the Narthex to gaze upon a miraculous picture of the Virgin. This ikon had been knifed by a priest who was enraged at being refused his supper after the usual time. Blood issued from the wound and slowly trickled down the picture. Instantly moved to repentance, he spent his remaining years in a little cupboard opposite. The hand that struck the blow withered, and was cut off at his request, as the Virgin had appeared to him in a dream, telling him that while she forgave him, she could never forgive his hand. This hand is preserved to-day in a box below the picture, in passive atonement.

The invaluability of Basil was demonstrated. Without his presence, my episode on Athos might prove fruitless. As it was, however, Basil was not only willing to join with me, but glad of my company. And so it was arranged that from to-day we should travel together. With the darkness, after a meal undistinguished by incident, we retired to our separate cells.

VATOPEDI.

Sleep was spasmodic ; periods of slumber broken by the realisation that my solitude was being disturbed. From all sides I was aware of the steady encroachment of animal life towards my prostrate form. The rigid code of Athos is sadly infringed by the wives and families of small and active creatures which abound within the very monastery cells. Throughout the night the invading horde of insect life conducted strategic operations over every obstacle. It is regrettable that the monastic law cannot be more strictly enforced. Cleanliness is, however, not one of the marked characteristics of the Athonite community. Each month the monks are blessed by a Superior, and Holy Water is sprinkled over their persons, which to wash off might be almost sacrilegious, in addition to destroying its efficacy.

PANTOCRATOR.

The Monastery of Pantocrator lies a few miles along the coast, south-east of Vatopedi. It is the poorest of the monasteries on Athos, and provides habitation for only twenty monks.

There exist on the Mountain two forms of autonomous government, Idiorrhythmic and Cenobian. Vatopedi was Idiorrhythmic ; Pantocrator is Cenobian. Here life is communistic, there being no private ownership of goods or property. Every possession of the monks is confiscated for the common purse and the monks eat and work together under the dictatorship of an abbot, who is elected by the community for life.

The Idiorrhythmic form of government allows the monk considerably more freedom. He may retain at least a part of his income, if he has any, and may employ servants to look after his room, which he may furnish himself. He lives his own life, doing his own cooking and eating in his own cell, only the barest necessities being supplied by the monastery. The governors of this community, three in number, are elected annually, undertaking the general administrative work and deciding minor questions of policy.

It must be stated here that although the greatest freedom is permitted in the Idiorrhythmic monasteries, it is often there that the monks practise the greatest severity. The hedonist is unknown. Nowhere in Athos may be found the equivalent of the rollicking, indulgent monk of mediæval Europe who rolled his lustful way through the scandalous pages of

FATHER GABRIEL

Balzac. The austere life of the monasteries is such that no one would dream of entering them to enjoy a life of laziness and gluttony. Prayers occupy a great portion of their day and night, so that the monks are never able to enjoy a good night's rest. Even at the services they must stand, and are only allowed to rest their arms on the projecting supports of the stalls which surround the lower half of the church. Anything approaching voracity is impossible, in view of the number of fast days which make up the Athonite year.

On these fast days, recognised by Idiorrhythmic and Cenobian monasteries alike, only one meal is eaten, from which fresh fish and oils are excluded. The absence of female creatures from the Mountain means that meat and dairy produce is unobtainable at any time, and many foods are peculiar, to say the least, to the Western palate. The staple meals seem to comprise salt fish, vegetables, fruit and octopus ; this last dish, eaten tepid, and having the consistency of rubber and the taste of linoleum, is an acquired taste. I never acquired it. The reason for the tepidity of the diet is that meals are invariably cooked before church service, and eaten after. Cooks, monks like the rest, attend the services and no oven arrangements seem to be made so that the food may be kept hot.

The Church of Pantocrator is painted that deep, chocolate colour the Byzantines loved. It is set within a white court studded with vivid Persian tiles, and sprouting orange trees from unexpected places.

The walls of the guest chamber, a hundred feet above the sea, proclaim in ruddy spots the eternal battle of man over insect. There is evident a pronounced contrast between the comparative luxury of Vatopedi and the poverty of Pantocrator. The installation of electric light by German engineers at Vatopedi had been one of the historical events of Athos before 1914. With the inception of the Great War, however, the electricians were called to the Fatherland while the task was scarcely complete, and if the resultant illumination is somewhat spasmodic and hazardous it makes at least some pretence to modern progress. Here at Pantocrator we must make do with the traditional oil lamps, one of which, of considerable age, was of unusually beautiful design. Little mention has been made, in any work that I know, of the numerous pieces of metalcraft and goldsmiths' art in Athos, though in many cases these must represent some of the finest and oldest examples extant. Of the more precious masterpieces preserved here, the majority were gifts from loose living Byzantine Emperors, as pious sops to their uneasy consciences.

STAVRONIKITA.

The journey from Pantocrator to Stavronikita is accomplished along the seashore in about one hour. Here is preserved a mosaic ikon, astonishing in itself, to which is attached a miraculous story. Painted ikons are a commonplace on Athos. As everyone who has visited an Orthodox Church knows, the most conspicuous feature of the interior is the large screen, or ikonastasis, which, covered completely with portraits of the Saints, cuts off the altar from the body of the church. The ikons of Athos are so numerous that the unusual naturally catches the eye. The interest of this particular ikon, dedicated to S. Nicholas, lies not in its subject-matter but in the medium of its execution. Mosaic pictures of such minute dimensions are exceedingly rare. Two others are preserved on

MONKS, ATHOS   67

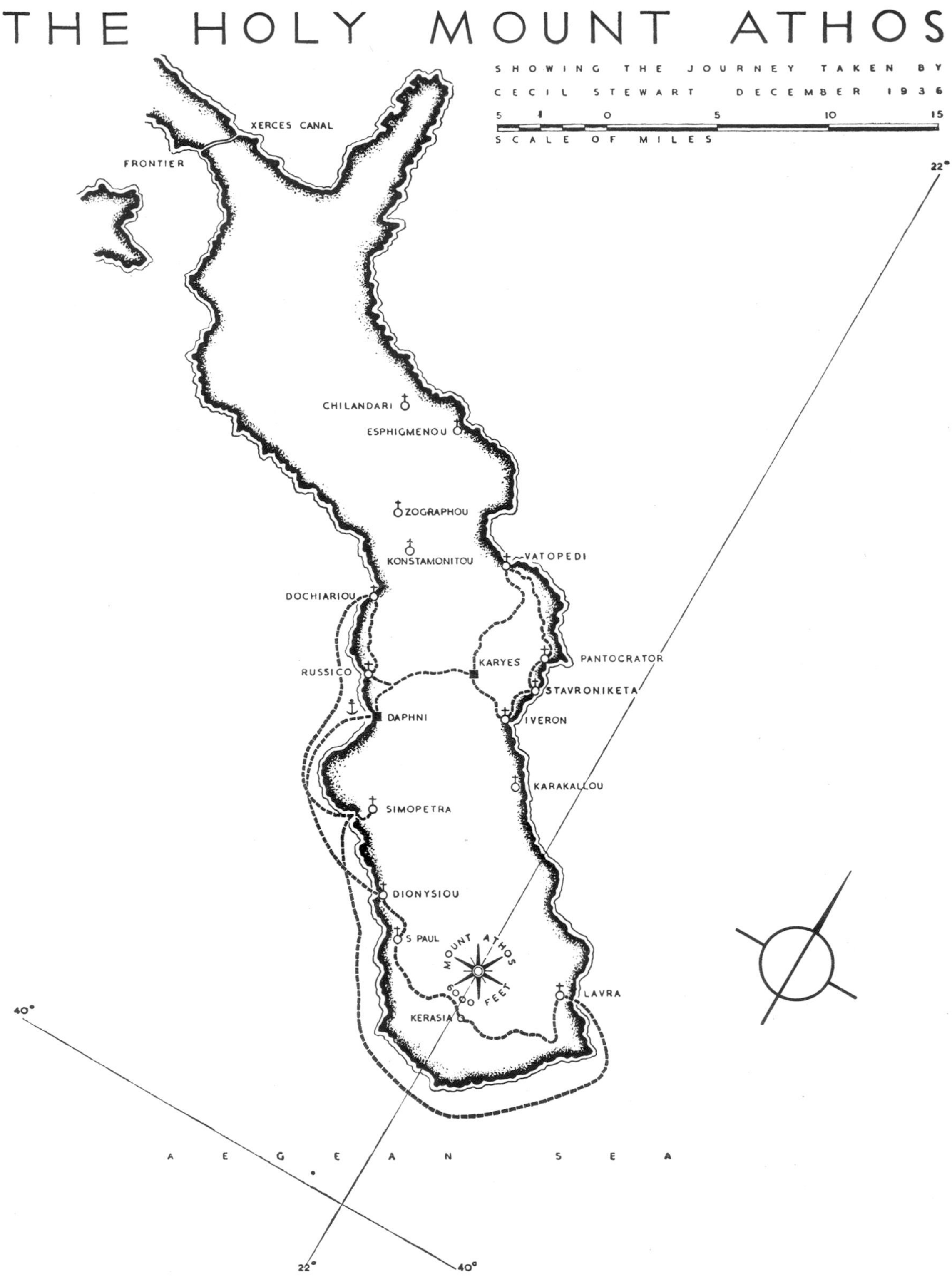
THE HOLY MOUNT ATHOS
SHOWING THE JOURNEY TAKEN BY
CECIL STEWART DECEMBER 1936
5 0 5 10 15
SCALE OF MILES
XERCES CANAL
FRONTIER
CHILANDARI
ESPHIGMENOU
ZOGRAPHOU
KONSTAMONITOU
VATOPEDI
DOCHIARIOU
KARYES
PANTOCRATOR
RUSSICO
STAVRONIKETA
DAPHNI
IVERON
KARAKALLOU
SIMOPETRA
DIONYSIOU
S PAUL
MOUNT ATHOS
6000 FEET
LAVRA
KERASIA
AEGEAN SEA
22°
40°

Athos and one in the Byzantine Museum at Athens. Carried out within an area incredibly small, every feature is beautifully delineated in a carefully patterned disposition of glass cubes, varying in colour, of which the largest is no more than an eighth of an inch square.*

The ikon, thrown into the sea during the Ikonoclastic period from we know not where, was found by the Patriarch Jeremias, illuminated with a supernatural glow, on the seashore where Stavronikita now stands. During the nautical episode, an oyster had attached itself securely to the features of S. Nicholas, and to-day a longish split is the only scar that remains in evidence. The shell, having been removed, now takes its part in the ritual of the refectory, where, surmounted by a loaf of bread, it is elevated and blessed ; then the bread so sanctified is divided and distributed amongst the monks, to their complete spiritual satisfaction.

Within the compass of Athos more sacred paintings and ikons, miraculous or otherwise, are preserved than anywhere else in the world. The most holy and venerated, like that of S. Nicholas, are covered with sheets of silver gilt, only the hands and faces being visible. Praying to ikons might be likened to idolatory, were it not for the firm belief that these pictures, animated in the minds of the devout, move through this Byzantine world as Divine Beings. In the whole of the Mountain there is present that peculiar atmosphere of the supernatural, so pronounced that it is necessary to approach these monks without scepticism. Only then can one hope to appreciate the deeper and finer side of Athos, where miracles are a daily occurrence.

Late in the afternoon it is time to go, as arrangements have been made that we should spend this night at Iveron.

" The sun will leave the Mountain within the hour," they told us.

" It is after eleven. You must hasten."

EN ROUTE.

Time on Athos is reckoned by the relationship between the sun and the Mountain. The day is divided into twelve " hours," from the time the sun first strikes the peak till the last ray leaves it. Thus the " hour " is shorter or longer according to the season. At sunset, or twelve o'clock, the gates of the monasteries are closed and admission is impossible.

Never have mules been so dilatory or so stubborn. With eyes glued upon the reddened peak, we urge on the imperturbable brutes. Arriving breathless at the gates, entry is barred by the black-robed figure of a monk, who, however, with a gesture of compassion, indulgently admits us, and we are led to the guest chamber as the gates clang behind us.

IVERON.

The Monastery of Iveron, of tenth-century foundation, is built close to the site where the Virgin was inadvertently carried while *en route* for Cyprus to pay a call on Lazarus. It is perhaps the largest on Athos, and presents the appearance of a mediæval town in miniature, with its crenellated walls of extraordinary height. These were heightened,

* There is an excellent example at the Victoria and Albert Museum.

in contradiction of accepted ideas, at the expense of the invading parties. It seems that an Emir, accompanied by a fleet of pirates, attacked and looted this monastery, driving the monks to the topmost tower. To complete the desecration, even the columns in the heart of the church were encircled by the cables from the ships in the bay, in the hope that the church might be pulled down. The monks prayed divine aid, and a great storm arose. All the vessels were destroyed except one, that in which the Emir, now terrified and repentant, asked for forgiveness and bequeathed enough money to prevent a similar disaster from ever happening again. In confirmation of the eternal durability of the church, if such be needed, there is set beneath the dome a circular slab inscribed in brazen letters : " I have set firm her columns and for all ages she shall not be shaken. George the Monk, Iberian and Founder." ★

The constant possibility of attack from the sea has to some considerable extent dictated the characteristic architectural form of the Athonite monasteries. Defence against plundering invasion decided that outside windows, other than the merest slits, should be avoided. It is only latterly, with the comparative security of the nineteenth century, that wooden penthouses have been built on the upper floors with galleries to relieve the severity of the façade. At the highest corner of the square formed by the impenetrable walls stands the tower, mediæval keep in appearance and fact, which of late has been commonly used to house the manuscripts and libraries of the monasteries. Generally, only one entry is possible to the courtyard, and that through a strongly defended gate which leads in some cases to a passage, fitted for further security with a series of armour-plated doors. The interior façade is more normally fenestrated. Here are disposed the windows of the cells, facing the courtyard, and doors which lead to painted galleries. At the ground floor, projecting into the courtyard, stands the re-fectory, facing the main door of the church. This building, like the churches, is adorned with frescoed patriarchs. The churches are invariably free-standing and follow the characteristic cross in square plan with the addition of a considerable narthex to accom-modate the large number of monks. They are complete in themselves and do not appear to take cognisance of the courtyard, whose disposition is dependent on the lie of the land. The result is that in some cases only a narrow lane is left between the main buildings and the churches, the galleries even overhanging, in some places, the leaden domes.

Set between the refectory and the principal church is the phiale, an octagonal unit surrounded by columns which carry a shell-like dome. This is the sacred well of the monastery, which on the first day of each month provides the water used for the blessing of all the inhabitants.

IVERON.

Shaving on Athos provides a constant source of embarrassment to me. Basil has capitulated and is producing an unseemly growth, to English eyes decadent, to say the least. One must keep up appearances even in this far-flung outpost of the Byzantine Empire, but, subjected to the disconcerting curiosity of the community at Iveron, the

★ Quoted by Dawkins, p. 264, " The Monks of Athos " (Allen & Unwin, 1936).

70

operation is performed with undue haste. A minor cut is sufficient to satisfy the monks of the complete futility of my efforts. Surely this is proof, if such were needed, that God had never intended his handiwork to be so disturbed. The monks allow even the hair upon their heads to grow unchecked, tying it, for convenience' sake, in a bun at the nape of the neck.

It would seem, at first, that the only remaining characteristic of the race which once bred heroes and philosophers is an insatiable curiosity. The Greek people still, as in the words of S. Paul, " spend their time in nothing else but either to tell, or to hear some new thing ". A source of petty irritation to the traveller on Athos, or in all Greece for that matter, is this constant inquisitiveness. On the other hand, the monks of Athos will spare no pains to help you all they can. They are lovable, kindly folk, whose simple sanctity and implicit faith can only be born of a great people. The keener and more brilliant intellectual thought may have gone, only the self-sufficiency and extraordinary tenacity of purpose remaining. But Athos, Holy Mountain, is the last living fragment of perhaps the greatest Empire the world has ever known and, as such, no lover of Byzantine Greece can leave it on one side.

Having the passport of the Holy Community, one is free to travel the length and breadth of the peninsula, to visit and receive the hospitality of all the monasteries without being asked for recompense of any sort, though a small donation to the guest-master is gratefully received. Mules are provided to carry you from monastery to monastery, and all that is expected is that you accept the normal customs of the Community, do not smoke near the church, pay due respect to the sacred relics, and attend at least one of the church services.

RUSSICO.

Nearly six thousand black robed, long-haired and bearded monks inhabit Athos to-day. All profess one common faith, the Greek Orthodox Church, and all obey the ruling of the elected Synod. Of this number a considerable proportion is drawn from outside Greece. There are on Athos monastic establishments housing Serbs, Bulgars, Rumanians and Russians. Of these four, the greatest community is Russian.

From the twelfth century till the collapse of the Romanoff dynasty, the government of Athos was continually disturbed by threats of Russian imperialism. The Monastery of Russico, the Russian dominion on Athos, was considerably enlarged by Catherine the Great, and became a Mecca, almost a new Jerusalem, catering for innumerable pilgrims with business-like efficiency. Early in the nineteenth century, a harbour, sufficient to accommodate a fair proportion of the Imperial Fleet, and a guest house—a veritable barracks—were built. The invasion of Russians to Athos was so great that by the close of the century they exceeded in number their Greek co-religionists. The danger of Athos falling completely into Russian hands was finally averted by the Great War and the Communist Revolution. From that time the number of Russians on the Mountain has steadily decreased, and the history of the now poverty-stricken community is distinguished by a single incident—that in which the Soviet Government in 1925 unsuccessfully proclaimed their right to the ownership of the Russian property on Athos, in contravention of the jurisdiction of the League of Nations.

72

Each monastery manifests its own distinguishing aura, but none more pronouncedly than Russico. Permeated with the utterly exotic character of religious Russia, the monastery is conspicuously different from its neighbours. It is no longer Greece ; here is coalesced, in some measure, the last flickering light of the Empire of all the Russias. With high, wrinkled boots beneath black cassocks, giant blondes move slowly about the courtyard, talking, but seldom gesticulating. Overhead, the green domed cupolas of the churches, surmounted with golden balls and wire crosses filled with lumps of coloured glass, complete a scene that could only be paralleled in Holy Russia or in the settings of " Prince Igor " or " Boris Godunov ".

From the Campanile the great bell booms out in melancholy rhythm. Three days ago a monk died, and to-day he will be laid to rest within the monastery precincts. As the monks age and their number diminishes, there seems little hope of the continuance of the monastery. In the church a pathetic quorum echoes over the dead man those mournful, tragic harmonies of unfathomable despair that only Russians could utter.

The graveyard is of minimum dimensions and accommodates only a few bodies at a time. After lying in an earthy bed for a couple of years, one is excavated to make room for each new arrival. The bones are kept in an old chest and the skulls, carefully docketed, are preserved on shelves in a sort of mausoleum. If a body is not decayed when exhumed, a stake is driven through the heart and the evil spirit exorcised in much the same way as in Bram Stoker's " Dracula," and for much the same reason.

There is little of architectural interest in the present buildings of Russico (for all can be surpassed in both extravagance and grandeur in Russia itself), and comparatively little of historical interest, as the entire monastery was built after Napoleon's retirement from Moscow.

RUSSICO.

The night was passed undisturbed, cradled in the comforts of a spring bed, an unusual luxury, my particular guest room being probably the finest in Russico. Here I slept, unaffected by the oleographs of the Czar and Czarina, in coronation attire, presiding royally at the bedhead. The monks on Athos have to some extent transferred their loyalty from the Byzantine Emperors to all the Kings and Queens of Europe, whatever their religious denomination, even George V of England being represented, amongst others, as a minor object of veneration.

Father Vasilius, the son of an ex-Cabinet Minister, trusts that I have slept well. Assuring him that I have never slept better, or in a more comfortable bed, I prepare to depart with Basil.

" Rasputin found it equally comfortable," remarks Vasilius.

I recalled having read that Rasputin had, on occasion, chosen Athos as a suitable place for his self-imposed exile from the Czarina, when he considered it politic. I had not, however, expected the dubious honour of sleeping on the bed so recently—as time goes on Athos—vacated by him.

DOCHIARIOU.

Architecturally, Dochiariou is the finest of the monasteries on Athos. Standing on the hillside rising steeply from the sea, the group of buildings is terraced in the form of a triangle, culminating, at the apex, in a tower of sixteenth-century construction. The courtyard is almost completely filled by the church, the largest on Athos, which possesses externally features almost Moldavian in character. The five domes, reaching above the tiled roofs and chimneys of the court, raised on tall, fluted drums and covered with lead in radiating pattern, are almost within reach of the gallery of the guest room.

DOCHIARIOU.

It had not been our intention to stay at Dochiariou. We were, however, half persuaded by the charm of the guest apartment overlooking the tall cupolas of the church to the sea beyond, as well as by our host's assumption that we would be resident for at least one night. But there seemed so many places to be visited that sadly we prepared to make our adieus.

"Could we hire a boat to take us to the Monastery of Simopetra?"

"It is impossible. This is the Day of S. Nicholas, and no ships sail these waters on this day."

This it seems is absolutely true, so we were inevitably persuaded.

The monastery is distinguished for its connections with the sea, and many stories are illustrated in fresco on the Phiale which tell of the seafaring episodes of this community. The monks of Athos are exceedingly well looked after by their Guardian Angels. It is they who find the wherewithal to build the monasteries; they protect the peninsula from plague and disaster; the masculine seclusion is preserved by their making the sea itself rise against possible feminine encroachment. It is the *pied-à-terre* of the Saints. On these sacred slopes Christ was led by the Devil to view from the summit the ancient Byzantium; to see "all the kingdoms of the world and the glory of them"; and there, Christ having spurned Satan for all time, the Angels visited Athos to minister unto Him.

GUEST MASTER AND THE AUTHOR, DOCHIARIOU

The Angels in latter-day history even stoop to protect the commercial interests of the Athonite Community. The instance which is recorded on the Phiale at Dochiariou deals with an adventurous band of sea-faring monks who, having visited a neighbouring possession and stowed aboard a cargo of corn, allowed their ship to be controlled thence-forward by the Archangels, who were present on board in the form of ikons. First, the ship was driven to famine stricken Barbary, where the welcome cargo brought handsome profit, and a second cargo of spices was taken on. This was carried to Constantinople, deprived of spices as a result of being at war with Barbary, and again a considerable profit accrued. Finally, after the ship's return to Dochiariou, it became known to the people of Barbary that the spices had been sold to their enemies, and a punitive force was sent to attack the monastery, only to be slaughtered by Michael and Gabriel in person.

Stories of the Saints and their activities on Athos are legion, and to give them the epithet myth or legend will offend the monks, who have absolute faith in their veracity. That these things did happen is to them undoubted, and even more surprising is their belief that similar occurrences might easily happen to-day. In fact there are tales of miraculous happenings, of nineteenth-century foundation, witnessed by living monks. To me, more astonishing than the tales is the fact that they are told to-day in precisely the same words as were used hundreds of years ago. These stories, which have been handed down by word of mouth at Athos, have been published by early travellers and do not appear to have been modified or amplified in any way.

Of the more recent supernatural events on the Mountain there is the tale of the miraculous painting of the Virgin at the Church of Prodromus. This painting, completed in the latter half of last century, was begun by a Rumanian painter, but as he could not carry out the work to his own satisfaction, he laid it away unfinished. Later, feeling inspired to complete the work, he took it out of the cupboard where it had lain, only to find, to his astonishment, that by a miracle the painting was complete and of great beauty. The picture accompanies a written testimony by the artist. On asking if I might photograph it, I was informed that efforts had been made before, but that even with long exposures the results had been complete failures, nothing whatever of the face of the Virgin coming out on the plate.★

The story of this ikon is described by an Anglican churchman, Mr. Riley, who obtained the information at first hand from a witness " who was acquainted with all the circumstances and appeared to be a man of true piety."

The Church of Dochiariou is dedicated to S. Michael, whose timely intervention made its erection possible. The interior is frescoed throughout and displays in the narthex the story of its origin. It seems that a peasant boy, miraculously directed, found great treasure ; so great, in fact, that he had to go to the Abbot to ask for assistance in carrying it to the monastery. Two monks offered their services and, reaching the spot, decided to appropriate it for their own nefarious purposes and tell the Abbot that this whole business of treasure trove was a figment of the boy's imagination and that he, in fear of retribution, had run away. The monks then tied a lump of marble which had covered

★ When my photographs were developed later in Salonika, I found that this particular film was hope-lessly over-exposed.

IKON, MOUNT ATHOS

78   IKON, MOUNT ATHOS

the treasure around the boy's neck and flung him over the cliffs. But the boy was sufficiently self-possessed to call upon divine aid as he made his involuntary descent into the sea.

The Archangel Michael, probably watching the whole affair from heaven and always ready in an emergency, swept down as the boy struck the water and bore him off to the old church. Meanwhile, the monks had returned and told their tale. In the morning, however, the boy was found, soaking wet, with the marble still around his neck, and so the monks were confounded, the treasure retrieved and the present edifice built. The marble boulder is to-day preserved in the church as one of its most cherished possessions.

SIMOPETRA.

It is a commonly accepted fact that the finest architecture answers two problems, that of pure functionalism and that of giving æsthetic satisfaction. Both are essential, and in point of fact it is often difficult to dissociate the two. The first can easily be proved in terms of practical needs, but the second is dependent upon that variable factor, taste. To-day it is becoming increasingly recognised that, broadly speaking, the purely functional becomes *ipso facto* a design of æsthetic significance. It might be better stated that good design is based upon the expression of utility.

Among the world's masterpieces, the Monastery of Simopetra, built only fifty years ago, must claim an important place. Backed by a thousand years of undisturbed traditional and functional design, this building comes to-day as a culminating achievement in an era which began with Sancta Sophia, perhaps the greatest church of all time.

Simopetra possesses those qualities of simplicity and directness of structural expression which are a characteristic of Byzantine design. This accomplishment is undoubtedly enhanced by the drama of its situation. As at the monasteries of Meteora, it is the approach and climb towards Simopetra that lends it that mystery which plays so important a part in all the finest Byzantine architectural expression. In taking advantage of the peculiarity of the sites, chosen for their impregnability, the Byzantines achieved a quality of composition comparatively unknown to the close adherents of Classic and Renaissance design, where the dictates of form, often of the most subtle proportioning and arrangement, limited and were even at times diametrically opposed to the consideration of functional structure and practical needs.

What, it may be asked, is true architectural expression? Is it simply that of truthful utilisation of materials? Or should it be an attempt to show externally the plan of a building by indicating the internal divisions and the various functions of the various units which compose the plan? Or should a building demonstrate its *raison d'être*? Of these possible standards of expression it is the last which must be considered of greatest importance, though a combination of all three might be deemed the ultimate achievement. Simopetra expresses in a direct and functional manner the structure, the plan and the purpose. In satisfying these dictates of architectural principle, this building, supremely satisfactory æsthetically, is the latest—perhaps the last—development in Byzantine art, ranking equal with, and surpassing many of, the greatest European architectural achievements.

SIMOPETRA, ATHOS

SIMOPETRA, ATHOS

SIMOPETRA, ATHOS

The approach from the sea is considerably more dramatic than from land. Rising sheer from the rock, the building, viewed from the several angles of the twisting, upward path, is staggering to say the least. Reaching its base, we are led in a final exertion up a path perched above rocky ravines on either side, to the entrance carved through the rock itself, which leads to a courtyard within the monastery walls.

While I have laid stress upon the functional attributes of Simopetra as an architectural entity, it must be appreciated that to some extent these functions which the monastery possesses are pure Byzantine tradition. At the far side of the monastery, enclosed within wooden walls and cut off from the galleries by a screen, are the latrines, traditional in extreme. A huge hole in the floor looks down to a cataract of rock, four hundred feet below. And it is here, bearing in mind a notice pinned outside insisting on accurate marksmanship, that one must stand like the statue of Rhodes to perform a feat only possible, with any degree of efficiency, to giants or experienced contortionists.

En Route.

While travel on land is made easy by the provision of mules at each monastery, a journey by sea involves the hiring of a lay workman whose financial acumen is, to put it mildly, iniquitous. Terms exorbitant in Basil's eyes having been finally agreed, the boat leaves the shore and we are at the mercy of the waves and, as I discover ten minutes later, at the mercy of the boatman. It appears that the sea is too rough, and he will only undertake the voyage at double the price. Basil points out that the state of the sea is the same as when we started, but this is of no avail, and before a conclusion is reached Basil turns a peculiar jaundiced hue, from which he does not recover throughout the journey. The trip from Simopetra to the Great Lavra nearly completes this circuit of Athos. On our left the Mountain rises six thousand feet sheer from the sea, and in its shadow we pass monasteries, watch towers and hermits' cells till, rounding the southern-most point, we reach, after five hours' sailing, the Great Lavra, senior monastery of Athos. Here Basil, although considerably weakened, with a conclusive gesture, effects a financial compromise.

Lavra.

Lavra, the prototype of all the monasteries on Athos, was founded by Athanasius, spiritual director of Nicephorus Phocas, the tenth-century Napoleon, who, conquering Crete, Mesopotamia, Syria and the Emirate of Aleppo, extended the Byzantine Empire to its maximum boundary. It had been the intention of Nicephorus to spend his latter days at Athos, the Elba of his choice, but now, over fifty and bewitched by a gay young thing called Theophano, he abandoned his ascetic impulse for the fleshpots of Byzantium.

It is difficult to assess how much of the original foundation remains. The antiquity of the principal church is undoubted, likewise of the two massive cypress trees planted by Athanasius and his disciple Euthimius. This battlemented town, by far the largest on Athos, contains no less than fifteen churches and preserves a host of relics, including five portions of the Holy Cross. Every monastery on Athos possesses some pieces, small or large, and Athos stands pre-eminent in Christendom with a total bulk of fifty-three and a half cubic inches. The Cross is said to have remained entire till the seventh century,

84

when, with encroachment on Palestine by the Infidels, it was divided into nineteen parts and distributed throughout the Empire to avoid its possible destruction. Rohault de Fleury, whose millimetric computations I have converted into inches, made a considerable study of the existing fragments of the True Cross, and calculates that the minimum possible volume of the original Cross was about 10,458 cubic inches, of which only 240 have survived.

The camera on Athos is still a comparative novelty and a source of considerable interest to the younger monks who, cut off from the outside world, insist on being photographed, and with surprising vanity take infinite pains to look their best. Such a monk was Stephen, who, seeing my camera, dashed indoors to appear five minutes later robed in Sunday best, complete with semandron and mallet, professional symbols, to pose before the Phiale of Lavra. Stephen is the equivalent of our own bellringer and upon him devolves the duty of marching around the courtyard with this shaped wooden plank which he strikes with the mallet in rhythm to announce the imminence of church service. The fifteenth-century Phiale at Lavra is the finest on Athos. A porphyry basin, seven and a half feet across, is surrounded by eight columns connected by tenth-century marble slabs at the base and above by brick arches which carry a lead-covered cupola, frescoed inside symbolically with the Baptism of Christ.

We were awakened at midnight by Stephen, attired as previously but for the less vain reason of announcing the midnight Mass. Within the church, dim and incense laden, the monks stand drooping over the crutch-like supports of the stalls, hour after hour, while the interminable service proceeds. The monks dare not fall asleep during service, for if they do a peculiar form of punishment is inflicted. One of their fellows takes a new lighted candle and quietly fixes it to the supporting arm of the stall. When the monk awakens and sees the candle, a customary atonement of continued acts of prostration, the duration varying according to the length of candle burnt, is insisted upon.

Within the narrow boundaries of the stall, the customary sequence of fresco meets the eye, this time illuminated by innumerable candles, lamps and bracket lights, and in the centre by the corona, a veritable ring of flames fifteen feet in diameter which, swinging gently, appears to animate the ethereal frescoed denizens which line the misty interior. Inevitably, with the first streaks of daylight striking across the hazy dome, the service terminates. The lamps and candles are extinguished and the ultimate prostration completed, while the monks slowly file out to begin another day.

EN ROUTE.

Lavra, it will be recalled, is situated on the eastern corner of the peninsula and comparatively close to the Peak itself. We left early on foot, having a considerable distance to go. For the first three hours we climbed up and around the southern spurs of the Mountain before we reached Kerasia, half a mile above the sea. In spite of greatcoats and gay woollen blankets provided by the beneficent monastery of Lavra, it was appallingly cold. The ground, covered in parts, like a mangy dog, with drifts of snow a foot deep, was hard and slippery. Kerasia is a dependency of the Monastery of Lavra and possesses a fire-place, an unusual accessory on Athos, which to-day, blazing fiercely, was welcomed as a means of thawing our tortured limbs. Outside, the wind howled

STEPHEN WITH SEMANDRON
Opposite: PHIALE, LAVRA

88   CHURCH INTERIOR, ATHOS

in the ravines, and through the window the Mountain towered, engulfed in a writhing blanket of cloud, impregnable to-day to the most foolhardy. The peak is about two and a half hours distant from Kerasia, in reasonable weather, and any hopes we had of ever achieving the chapel at the summit were finally damped by Father Andrea. Instead, circulation being restored by ouso and Russian tea, we directed our attentions and our feet towards Dionysiou, the ultimate goal.

DIONYSIOU.

Like Simopetra, Dionysiou is perched upon a rock, having the living quarters at the uppermost storeys, but the evenness of the fenestration is here disturbed by many additions made outwards, whole ranges of cells projecting into the air, upheld by match-like supports which in their turn depend upon lower storeys similarly carried. The whole effect is picturesque in the extreme, the appreciation of which is tempered on entering the guest chamber, a hundred and fifty feet directly above the cliffs and the sea, by the realisation that it is the peculiar precariousness of these apartments which give that charm.

At seven I was washed, dressed and prepared for this my last day on Athos. Entering the kitchen in anticipation of a morning cup of coffee, Father Gabriel greets me.

" Kalimera sas—good morning, have you slept well ? "

I confess that sleep was spasmodic, disturbed as it was by the howling gale outside. The morning is still cold, and with a sly look the Father produces, in addition to the coffee, a glass of ouso. This ouso, he explains, distilled from grapes off vines planted by Dionysious himself, is very strong. Recklessly I swallow, and a host of fire engines tears down my throat, torture only being slightly abated by following the course with pints of icy water.

Basil, called in to witness my final agony, and by way of fraternal correction, proceeded, in complete disregard of the tears streaming down my face, to translate Gabriel's tale of the particular vine that caused my present anguish.

Dionysious, a young man at the time of his first visit to the Mountain, happened to pick up a vine shoot from the roadside, and, to protect it from the sun, placed it in the thigh bone of a bird. Through this it very shortly grew, so that, afraid it might wither, he placed the plant and bone inside a second bone, that of a lion. And it grew and grew and grew, filling the second bone. This time he found the bone of an ass to accommodate his increasing burden, and in that form it was carried to Athos, to be planted and ultimately to produce magnificent grapes from which Dionysious distilled the first wine. And the whole point of the story is this, that, when a little wine was drunk the recipients sang like birds, when they had a little more they grew strong like lions, and having yet more, behaved like asses.

Stories such as this and others I have related all go to form that peculiar pattern of Athos. A pattern incomprehensible at first, which can only be appreciated after discarding natural laws and current ideas. This unique haven of countless Angels and Saints has maintained for the thousand years of its existence an identical purpose and idealism, while the surrounding world has passed it by as no longer intelligible or significant to contemporary life.

With the evening, the sun sets behind the golden rim of sea and lingers on the snowy

REFECTORY, DOCHIARIOU

DIONYSIOU, MOUNT ATHOS

peak of Athos. From the guest-room, a vantage point high above the land and the water, the lights of the port of Daphni shine on the darkening waves, paling to insignificance as the stars intensify in the darkness and the water turns from silver to lead. As I look out the window and see the spangled sky, and the clouds riding up the Mountain, and the water lapping silver against the blackened cliffs, I recall the enchantment of these last few days, cut off from the world as in a dream. Enchantment it must be. Only so beguiled can the full dignity and beauty of Athos be recognised and only so can the import of its grandeur be appreciated and understood. I will never forget these days.

EN VOYAGE.

The steamer comes to rest in the bay of Daphni. The same rowing boat that brought me now takes me away. Basil waves from the shore.

Once on board the atmosphere is changed. Shingled heads and high heels with soprano cries demand pink gins and side cars at an improvised cocktail bar. The steward tells me the world's news; of how King Edward VIII has abdicated, that the Crystal Palace has been burnt down, and that Zaharoff, Greek millionaire munitions maker, is dead. But as we steam out my thoughts and eyes return to Athos. Basil, with a final flutter of handkerchief, disappears. As the ship steams from the port, the monasteries Dochiariou, Russico, Simopetra and Dionysiou return to view before the mountain, clear and sparkling in the sun. We turn to starboard, till, rounding the second finger of Chalcidice, all is lost.

END OF THE FIRST PART

CHAPTER FIVE

NO STUDY OF ANY ARTISTIC EPOCH CAN BE COM-
plete if the historical and geographical background is disre-
garded, and no comprehensive study of Christian art can be
undertaken without some consideration of the religious impulse
which gave it birth.

Until officially recognised by Constantine in A.D. 313, the
Christians, from the Roman point of view, were a comparatively unpopular lot, worshipping their unknown God in underground haunts on the outskirts of Rome, and digging at the
very foundations of paganism by converting the slaves to a
teaching which informed them that eternal bliss was an easier
accomplishment for them than their masters . . . " it is easier
for a camel to go through the eye of a needle than for a rich
man to enter the Kingdom of God ". . . . The Christians, too,
extravagantly promised perpetual happiness to all and sundry
who would accept a most strange doctrine. One was asked to believe that a certain
Jesus of Galilee, whom for reasons of policy the Romans had seen fit to crucify, had
been immaculately conceived by a Virgin, Mary, and was the Son of Jehovah, God of
the Jews.

The Romans had tolerated the Jews, as their religion accepted the legal authority of
Rome and seemed to be confined within the limits of their own community. But the
Christian offshoot believed the conversion of others to be its supreme duty and as such
was not to be endured by the pagan. It seemed, however, that the Christians, filled
with divine fire, were quite prepared to die for their faith, and it was undoubtedly this
marked characteristic which first attracted Constantine, the militant Emperor of the West.
They knew how to die.

The Gods of the Empire had retired to leave Rome to its fate. Rome was falling
into dissolution. The Emperor Diocletian had split the Empire, giving authority to
four rulers as far apart as England, Serbia, Syria and Italy. In England Cæsar Constantius
Chlorus, after one year of power, was engaged in preparing an expedition against the
Picts when he died at York. His son Constantine was publicly acclaimed Emperor by
the troops on 25th July, 306, and then began a period of war, diplomacy and intrigue
which after eighteen years was to find Constantine sole ruler of the Roman Empire.

By degrees Constantine's leanings towards Christianity were made evident. Christianity
began to have similar privileges to other religions. As the actual date of Christ's birth
was unknown, it was fixed as identical with that of Mithra, a more powerful and far
more ancient religion, having much in common with Christianity, so that the Christians
could celebrate undisturbed while the heathens commemorated in the circus.

With the Edict of Milan in A.D. 313 Constantine finally placed Christianity on an

94

equal footing with paganism and by easy stages the way was clear for Christianity to replace it. Of all religions Christianity was the most amenable and least conservative. The adoption of rites similar to those of paganism made the change surprisingly easy. The pageantry of the temple, the feasts of the Gods and the divine tokens were substituted by the ceremonial of the Church, Christmas holidays and Easter eggs. The blood lust which had been satisfied by the massacre of Christians at the Colosseum was mitigated by the burning of heretics. The pomp and circumstance of Imperial Rome need not be disturbed one jot. Christianity could give the people everything they had before and could in addition promise to its adherents life everlasting.

Step by step the mysteries of the pagan religions were adapted to become a part of the Christian story. The Resurrection of Christ from a rock tomb followed the precedent of Mithra, also raised from a rock tomb. The turning of water to wine had already been accomplished by Dionysus, son of Zeus, who similarly rode upon an ass and fed multitudes in the desert. Like Poseidon, Christ walked upon the water, and like the greater Gods was born of a virgin.

But Rome was no longer the centre of political gravity. In these latter days the vast assemblage of public buildings housing a pauperised population of slaves was merely the nominal mistress of the world, and a source of considerable expense and trouble without even commercial importance.

With the steady decline of the influence of Rome, the cultural and economic heart of the Empire was shifting eastward, and it remained for Constantine to fix on the exact spot on which to found the new seat of government for the first Christian Empire. After a period of procrastination and indecision, and ultimately with divine aid, the ancient town of Byzantium was chosen, and here on foot, spear in hand, Constantine defined the boundaries of the future Constantinople. It was the inauguration of an epoch which was to endure for over a thousand years and to preserve throughout the darkest ages of mediæval Europe the cultural heritage of Greece, Rome and the Orient.

The importance of Constantinople as a cultural and economic centre cannot be over-emphasised. Situated on a promontory of enormous strategic value, Constantinople became in a very short time the commercial nucleus of the known world. It controlled the only sea route from Russia to the Mediterranean, and at Scutari, on the opposite bank, the caravans from Persia and China unloaded. From east and west travellers and traders, princes and painters, flocked to the new city. Constantinople absorbed the distinctive qualities of them all and disseminated throughout the whole of the imperial dominions the legacy of Byzantium.

For centuries it successfully repulsed the onslaughts of Huns, Saracens, Bulgarians, Turks and Serbs. In making territorial acquisitions it claimed, as the first Christian Empire, the sublime privilege of conferring salvation upon the conquered. From Constantinople, on the divine wave-length, messages were sent to prove to the enemy that defeat by Constantinople would virtually be an advantage, not a loss. But tragically this Empire was to suffer its greatest defeat from Christians beyond the pale of Constantinople. Marching ostensibly to free the Holy Sepulchre from the infidels, the Crusaders, instead of sticking to their job, attacked and looted Constantinople, ultimately to leave it as easy prey for the eventual Mohammedan onslaught. On Friday, the 1st June, 1453, the city fell to Mohammed II, and it was not long before the last remnants of the Empire were under Turkish dominion. So terminated the history of Constantinople as a source of inspiration to European civilisation. But the seeds already sown flourished with surprising magnificence in countries outside the original empire ; in Russia the capitulation of Constantinople prefaced an epoch of fantastic grandeur, which echoed at Kiev and Moscow the imperial majesty and splendour of the Byzantine Empire. An epoch which reached its zenith in the sixteenth century in the Church of S. Basil at Moscow and endured to a lesser degree until the revolution of 1917. In Rumania the churches of Sukivita and Voronet are amongst the greatest examples of Byzantine achievement, though built two centuries after the collapse of Constantinople. Far and wide the influence of Constantinople prevailed. In Greece we have seen that influence persist to the present day. Simopetra, although only fifty years old, must be one of the finest examples of Byzantine architecture. S. Basil at Moscow is fundamentally a Byzantine creation, though it was scarcely likely to have been built by craftsmen from Constantinople. In the same way, throughout Western Europe the plunder of the Crusades proved a constant source of inspiration to mediæval craftsmen, and exerted an influence to which Gothic and Renaissance art is considerably in debt.

CONSTANTINOPLE.

It would be a singularly insensitive voyager who, approaching Constantinople for the first time, did not feel some thrill of anticipation. To me particularly Constantinople typifies that supreme occasion in world history when East and West joined hands, to produce for a period an art and architecture unsurpassed before or since. As such it takes its place as the goal and zenith of this soliloquy and no number of minarets or other Turkish delights can detract from this primary conception. Constantinople can be like no other city in the world. Silhouetted on a promontory stretching from Europe, the multi-domed citadel gives on approach a sensation never to be forgotten. The good ship " Excambion " rounds the corner of the Sublime Porte and casts anchor in the Golden Horn. Just across the way is Asia, and All The Glamour Of The East is accessible from here by cheap excursion every twenty minutes.

SANCTA SOPHIA.

Sancta Sophia has received the attention of so many writers and historians for well over a thousand years that any ecstatic eloquence of mine would be at the cost of reiteration and so may be taken as read. The church as it stands to-day is unique, the supreme achievement of Byzantine art.

It is customary to regard the creation of nearly every architectural entity as a natural development in a sequence of architectural evolution. Thus the Romans adopted with modifications the work of their predecessors the Greeks. The Romanesque builders developed the legacy of Rome. Gothic architecture was consequential to Romanesque. And so on. But in the Eastern Empire a remarkable development had taken place. The Greek builders in Constantinople devised a system of construction entirely new and unparalleled in the history of the world. They created an architectural composition which for sheer size and magnificence is beyond compare. Raised upon pendentives a hundred and fifty feet above the earth and covering an area of over eleven thousand super feet, the great dome of Sancta Sophia must rank pre-eminent in the architectural accomplishments of man.

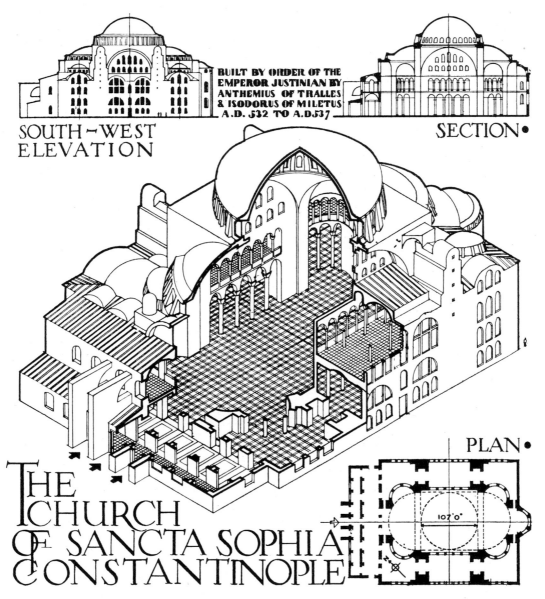

SOUTH~WEST ELEVATION

BUILT BY ORDER OF THE EMPEROR JUSTINIAN BY ANTHEMIUS OF TRALLES & ISODORUS OF MILETUS A.D. 532 TO A.D.537

SECTION•

THE CHURCH OF SANCTA SOPHIA CONSTANTINOPLE

PLAN•

107'0"

Perhaps the greatest problem which confronts the designer of vaults and domes is the outward thrust which these structural units exert upon the supporting walls. In the west the difficulty was somewhat clumsily overcome by the expedient of propping the outside walls where required by a series of petrified shores. These props and struts, known as buttresses, characterise all Gothic architecture. The Greeks, however, with complete mastery of form, evolved in Sancta Sophia, with domes and semi-domes, a splendid system of construction which contained the thrust and counter-thrust within the building itself. The great dome is supported with so little apparent effort, like a canopy in space, that Procopius, contemporary with its construction, suggested that it seemed to hang by a golden cord from heaven. Sancta Sophia was completed in A.D. 537, and though almost the earliest building in the Byzantine epoch nothing even approaching it in size and grandeur was ever built again. A miracle of space, shadowless and undefined, the Church of Sancta Sophia, while originating a constructional formula which prevailed on a smaller scale throughout the centuries of the Empire, remained for all time the consummate achievement of Byzantium.

On Friday, the 1st of June, 1453, Constantinople fell into the hands of the Turks, and Mohammed, riding a white charger, entered Sancta Sophia and, looking towards Mecca, gave thanks to Allah. Every subsequent Friday, till the advent of Mustapha Kemal, the Caliph, Shadow of God on Earth, rode likewise across the Golden Horn to Sancta Sophia, there to pray. But His Excellency Mustapha Kemal Pasha proclaimed Islam, this theology of an immortal Arab, a dead myth, suitable perhaps for the nomads of the desert, but hopeless for the modern progressive state. Accordingly the Caliphate was abolished, and not long after the Mosque of Sancta Sophia, thus freed from Mohammedanism, became a museum. To-day the impress of nearly five hundred years is being removed. The great green discs with golden Arabic characters which proclaimed its function as a mosque now stand stacked in the aisles awaiting removal. The precious mosaics so long hidden by layers of whitewash will soon return to view. Far up in the semi-dome above the altar the great face of Christ Pantocrator, His hand raised in eternal benediction, is slowly being uncovered. When all that remains is finally displayed, a clearer idea will be obtained of how great this Christian church must have been.

In its hey-day it was filled with treasure of incredible value. Across the eastern end stretched an iconastasis of silver and gold with doors of ivory and cedar and amber. Behind stood the altar, an astonishing creation, cast from a mould which was filled with a veritable soup of gold and silver into which were flung with reckless abandon cupfuls of the most precious gems of the Empire. On its face was set the fabulous Byzantine pearl. The church contained forty censers of pure gold, the Imperial Crowns of the Emperors, a score of inlaid crosses, bejewelled reliquaries, silver candelabra and priceless gold and silver chalices and patens ; and relics large and small, ranging from the table at which Christ celebrated the Last Supper to His swaddling clothes, from the doors of Noah's Ark to the tears of the Virgin—naïvely described by a contemporary as resembling pearls.

For hundreds of years Constantinople and the Church of Sancta Sophia received the tribute due to it from a mighty empire. It was the wealthiest and most splendid city in the world. Rome had never known such grandeur and was forced to take a second place. The kings and queens reigned at Constantinople, while the knaves cherished in Rome that ace of spiritual primacy which had been undisputed from the time of its

SANCTA SOPHIA, CONSTANTINOPLE (EXTERIOR) 99

SANCTA SOPHIA, CONSTANTINOPLE (INTERIOR)

Petrite origin. Rome, bitterly jealous of the worldly supremacy of Constantinople, and goaded beyond endurance at the decision of the Patriarch at Constantinople to side against her with Egypt over a spiritual bone of contention regarding the nature of the Second Person of the Trinity, inaugurated a rival empire in the West. Charlemagne was crowned Emperor at Rome and later, at the fanatical call of Peter the Hermit, the Eastern Empire was invaded in the guise of the Crusades. Constantinople, then fighting to preserve her eastern frontiers from the steady advance of the Seljuk Turks, was in dire peril.

The professed desire to free Jerusalem from the Infidels was forgotten. " If you do not care to fight for these, and gold will tempt you more, you will find more of it at Constantinople than in the whole world, for the treasures of its basilicas alone would be sufficient to furnish all the churches of Christendom, and all their treasures together cannot amount to those of Sancta Sophia, whose riches have never been equalled even in the Temple of Solomon." Thus wrote Alexius Comnenus to Robert, Count of Flanders, when asking for the assistance of the West to fight the Infidels.

Constantinople fell in 1204 and the city was looted on a scale unparalleled in history. From Sancta Sophia the gold and the treasures were removed in cartloads, a fair quantity of which was ultimately to reach the Treasury of the Vatican at Rome. One of the Crusaders writes : " It is the belief of me, Geoffrey Villehardouin, Marechal of Champagne, that the plunder of this city exceeded all that has been witnessed since the creation of the world."

Denuded of its gilded trappings, Sancta Sophia is still the outstanding architectural achievement of the age. That plunder inspired development in the West is acknowledged. Isolated churches were built in Western Europe by Byzantine refugees, following the same constructional principles. Perigueux in France, S. Mark, Venice, and Charlemagne's Church at Aix-la-Chapelle are isolated cases in which the Byzantine origin can be traced, but nowhere was anything equal in size or magnificence ever attempted, for the simple reason that it required an ingenuity and knowledge of construction beyond the powers of any Western builders.

S. JOHN OF THE STUDION.

In the early story of the Christian Church there exist no records of any representation of Christ or the Saints other than symbolically. Of the likeness and appearance of Christ there is not one syllable or reference in the Gospels or in the literature of His time. The early Christians, influenced by their Hebrew forefathers, must have felt a considerable repugnance to representation in any form of the spiritual entity of the Lord and His fellows. But the use of symbols was a commonplace which did not offend even the heathens. The Christians accepted pagan symbols and infused them with divine significance ; the Cross, the Anchor, the Palm Branch, the Lamb and the Vine, derived from paganism, became filled with a new religious import. It was not till the year 691 at Constantinople that the Council in Trullo of a hundred and two canons declared " that henceforth Christ was to be publicly exhibited in the figure of a man not a lamb." So for a period the picture was to supersede the emblem. However, with the advent of Leo the Isaurian to the Imperial throne the decision was reversed. He, stung by the jibes of the Jews and Mohammedans, who called the Christians idolators, and honestly wishing to free Christianity from superstition, called together three hundred and thirty-eight bishops who, after six months' persuasion, decided that after all pictures of the Saints were " a blasphemy against the fundamental dogma of our salvation."

Here in the Monastery of S. John of the Studion, which is our chief concern at the moment, memorable scenes were enacted. Challenging the right of the Emperor to intervene as he had done in this purely religious matter, the monks of Studion on Palm Sunday, A.D. 815, processed around the monastery carrying their ikons aloft in triumphal defiance. Their efforts proved, at least temporarily, unavailing, and it was not till the year 842 that a council of three hundred and fifty bishops was held, passing a vote in favour of pictorial depiction and at the same time dictating to some extent the convention of saintly representation which has been adhered to throughout the centuries and which has produced the characteristic Byzantine style.

The church of the Monastery of Studion was the oldest surviving in Turkish Constantinople. Built in 463, it endured comparatively intact up till the present century, when, under an unusual weight of snow, the wooden roof collapsed. To-day, a ruin open to the elements, interest centres on the floor, which is remarkably well preserved. Marble tessaræ, ranging in infinite gradations of colour, are inlaid spiral fashion around slabs of verd antique and brown trachite. Marble mosaic was a commonplace of pre-Christian art in Greece and Rome, where it was constantly in demand because of its durability and decorative value. Pictures of extraordinary detail were created for the floors of Pompeii, where the art reached perfection, but it is to the early Christians that recognition is due for the promotion of this form of decoration from the floors to the walls. At the same time, they accepted the traditional mode of floor covering in their churches, though never emulating the achievements of the Romans in that sphere. On the floors of the Church of Studion the general appearance is somewhat disturbed by numerous upturned flowerpots which spot the surface, and it is not until the guide carefully lifts one up that one understands. For under each spot is a delicate piece of incised carving and the pots are umbrellas protecting them from rain and frost. So one wanders round lifting each cover in turn, displaying little animals, birds, and foliage compositions, each one seeming more perfect than the last, till with regret the final pot is lifted and the guide's impatient itching palm pacified.

KARIEH DJAMI.

The early Christians, forced to worship in the obscure and badly illumined catacombs, launched the new craft of wall mosaic in the second century A.D. Mosaic was chosen as decoration for the very good reason that it alone, in surface adornment, is enhanced by the minimum amount of light. Those vitreous cubes, which in some peculiar way sparkle and glitter with inherent brilliancy behind a candle flame, would in light of day be severely toned and modified by the surrounding brightness. In the middle of the fourth century, when Christianity was released from its underground domains, the architects designing the new churches took particular care to ensure just that minimum of light necessary to illuminate the glistening walls. And there can be no doubt that it

S. SAVIOUR (KARIEH DJAMI), CONSTANTINOPLE

S. SAVIOUR (KARIEH DJAMI), CONSTANTINOPLE

is that strange, almost unbegotten light which pervades the mosaiced churches of the Byzantine Empire that lends them their particular mystery and charm. Byzantine architecture, with its system of dome and vault construction, gave the ideal surface for mosaic decoration. Its curved internal forms reflect light from each covering cube and facet to considerably greater effect than on a flat wall with even illumination.

In the study of mosaic decoration, two main periods can be clearly distinguished, before and after the iconoclastic episode. Of the early period one example, that of S. Demetrius in Salonika, is outstanding in Eastern Europe. At a later stage in this chronicle Rome and Ravenna will furnish more. The period is distinguished by its constant elevation of the Imperial Court to heavenly majesty amongst the angels. The Christ is beardless, like Apollo, and the human rather than the spiritual side is made apparent. The Virgin, originally simply attired sitting on a wooden bench, is, at the period of highest development, enthroned on a sparkling replica of the Byzantine throne, and robed in much the same bejewelled garments that the Empresses of that period would have worn. The Apostles stride the golden heavens in togas, like Senators of the Imperial Government. Thus are the mighty risen, and their effectiveness as governors of a mighty empire must be considerably enhanced in the public eye by their apparent resemblance to the Heavenly Body.

Of the later period, the mosaics of Karieh Djami are the last and supreme achievement of this Byzantine craft. The dignity of the Court by now established, it remains to enhance the spiritual aspect of the heavenly story. The saintly denizens are no longer human of aspect, and thus the corporeality which had so offended the iconoclasts and image-breakers was avoided. The figures are flat symbols elongated to unhuman proportion and are there primarily to illustrate the Gospel story. Lettering, spasmodic at first, now plays an integral part both as decoration and instruction. Every picture tells a story, and on this depends to no small degree the merit of the craft from a Byzantine viewpoint. In those days of comparative illiteracy, before the art of the book was an accomplished fact, the spiritual education of the people depended almost entirely on these illustrated buildings, which Ruskin likens to " a vast illuminated manuscript, bound with alabaster instead of parchment, studded with porphyry pillars instead of jewels, and written within and without in letters of enamel and gold ".

The mosque known as Karieh Djami, originally dedicated to S. Saviour, is of Justinian foundation. It was considerably restored about the same time as the Norman Conquest, and incidentally, the immigration of English refugees to Constantinople. The bulk of the mosaics which adorn the interior are of fourteenth-century workmanship, and were brought to light for the Kaiser's delectation when he visited the city at the end of the last century.

They were the last word in Byzantine mosaic. Never again was this art to be attempted by Byzantine craftsmen. The millennium of the Empire was drawing to a close with this supreme effort. A new spirit had entered Byzantine art, a spirit which, migrating after the collapse of Constantinople, survived impecuniously in the form of fresco painting. For mosaic was essentially the decoration of the wealthy, and as such was the product of prosperity. With the fall of the Empire and the survival for a brief period of the

Dependency of the Morea, the decorative ideals, transmuted to mosaic at Karieh Djami, prevailed at Mistra as fresco.

And with that final flourish Byzantine art retired into obscurity. It is not till comparatively recent times that the full import of Byzantine painting has been appreciated. Robert Byron and Talbot Rice have demonstrated, in " The Birth of Western Painting ", by means of adjacent reproductions, that the Renaissance of Italian painting is in considerable debt to Byzantine art. The origins of the Primitives of Siena are now known ; the Byzantine inspiration of Giotto, Cimabue and El Greco is to-day acknowledged.

The mosaics of Karieh Djami show scenes from the lives of Christ, Mary and Joseph, which are commonplace in Orthodox history but not so frequently publicised in the pictorial representations of the Roman Catholic Church. Although some have been severely damaged by the Infidels, sufficient remain to give a very good idea of what the church must have looked like in its prime. Certain scenes are outstanding. There is the delightful depiction of Joseph, bearing an expression of bewildered astonishment on being informed by an Angel that his betrothed will shortly bear a son. Of considerable interest, too, is the lunette over the main entrance which portrays Theodore Metochites presenting to Christ a model of the church, and incidentally giving us a very good idea of how gorgeous the costume of that time must have been. He wears an astonishing bulbous turban which was presented to him by the Emperor as a mark of special distinction. But of all the scenes depicted the most striking is the representation of the Nativity, which for sheer quality of colour and originality of composition surpasses all the others. Here in a manger is the Infant Jesus, lit by a ray of light which strikes down directly from Heaven, while an ox and an ass peer over the swathed Child. Below this the Virgin reclines unconcernedly on a couch. To the right, at the back, a group of interested shepherds are informed of the glad news by an Angel, while in the foreground Joseph huddles in a corner gazing in solitude at two women who bathe the Child in the left-hand corner.

The whole composition pays little heed to the laws of perspective, and its naïve expressionism can only be paralleled in the early Giottos and in the present trend.

GUL DJAMI.

Distances in Constantinople appear absurdly small measured on the map, but measured by sheer effort and exhaustion are considerable. Armed with a map, the Church of S. Theodosia, now the Mosque of Gul Djami, seemed comparatively easy of access and in a direct line with the second bridge spanning the Golden Horn. Crossing the first, and plodding for about two miles over that peculiar configuration of mud and cobbles which never deserved the appellation road, the city walls were reached and passed. The second bridge simply did not exist, and the map was no more to be trusted than its creators.

Retracing the journey, the Church of S. Theodosia is found up a side alley which had been passed an hour before. Now it is called the Rose Mosque, and with that designation the culminating agony of the church's history is perpetuated. On the night of the 28th May, 1453, the siege of Constantinople had reached its crisis. Dawn would witness the survival or collapse of the city. Throughout the day the panicking population

S. THEODOSIA (GUL DJAMI), CONSTANTINOPLE 107

invoking divine aid, had processed the streets. Within the Church of S. Theodosia the greatest and wealthiest ladies of the Empire held solemn vigil throughout the night, until the morning of the fateful day. Suddenly, at eleven o'clock, the cavalry of Mohammed the Conqueror surrounded the church, battered down the doors and dragged off the shrieking women as prisoners of war.

It was the season when the scent of roses mingled with the less pleasant odours of the mediæval city. The church was everywhere decked with the flowers in memory of the day when Theodosia, opposing the iconoclastic policy of Leo, was put to death by an infuriated soldier. The picture of the church, thus embowered with roses, was so vivid that ever since it has been called Gul Djami, the Rose Mosque.

The transformation of this and nearly all the city's Byzantine churches into mosques has been so considerable that their interest to-day is comparatively insignificant. Every Christian symbol was overlaid with the mask of Mohammedanism. The walls, covered with whitewash, were only relieved by the intricate arabesques of puritan Islam. The altars and pulpits were supplanted by the steep austere mimbars, where the Imam persists in noonday supplication, though the number of the Faithful is dwindling to insignificance. As in Russia, only the old and the poor still cling to the faith of their forefathers.

The state, originally a religious polity, is now a secular republic. Known up till the time of the Great War as "The sick man of Europe," Turkey was inevitably disintegrating. Mustapha Kemal, within an astonishingly short time, achieved the dissolution of the old regime and the initiation of the new. At a meeting of the Assembly Kemal issued his ultimatum : "Academic discussion leads nowhere," he proclaimed. "It would be of assistance if everyone in this Assembly were to find this view a proper and natural one." He even went so far as to suggest that in the event of stubbornness on the part of members, "some heads might have to be cut off." That would be very unfortunate, and with the acknowledgment of a few hands the President declared Kemal's motion carried unanimously.

The Caliph, Shadow of God on Earth, was bundled into a cab with a bag of clothes and a few pounds for his fare to Switzerland and driven across the frontier. A couple of days later the princes and princesses of the Sultan's court followed suit. The Ottoman Empire was dead, the Revolution achieved.

Only the pathetic remnants of the Faithful persist. Deprived to-day even of the fez, which had made their repeated prostrations a comparatively easy accomplishment, they make a tragic sight with tattered caps, reversed for convenience' sake, with the peak behind like decrepit racing cyclists.

The fez, though introduced only a hundred years ago as a substitute for the turban, had occasioned an outcry at the time which was only surpassed in vehemence when Kemal ordered western headgear to take its place.

But if much has been lost in this westernising process, there is one place at least where the despondent traveller might hope to recapture some of the colour and glamour of the East—the Grand Bazaar ! The name may conjure up in the mind a vision of the biggest, brightest Woolworths in the world, or suggest the sort of thing the ladies of the parish organise to pay for mending the leak in the vicarage roof, or you may see it as an Arabian Nights' extravaganza of brilliant and bewildering colour; mounds of unbelievable fruits, bowls of magical sweetmeats, cascades of rich silks and exquisite embroideries, and stalls whose awnings are rare and beautiful carpets. The Grand Bazaar is, in fact, a combination of all these things. It is as well organised as Woolworths, displays as much junk as the Church Hall, and at the same time offers the genuine article to him whose time and pocket-book are both unlimited.

CONSTANTINOPLE.

There is a danger, in a work of this nature, of exaggerating the things that interest and turning a blind eye on the more obvious or unsavoury facts as they present themselves. One has built up in the imagination a picture in such glowing colours that when the reality is confronted one is liable to pass it by. One can walk over excrement and slime in Constantinople, and it is impossible not to, as though on fabled Eastern carpets. One's mind is so filled with the fantastic splendour of the city's history that it seems almost incredible that it should have sunk so low. The Sweet Waters of Europe, the Sublime Porte, the Golden Horn and so forth, are singularly deceiving titles and no matter how hard one may try, the reality just won't fit the legend.

For the first few days the tourist can be so completely immersed in his Baedeker or its equivalent that he can see great monuments, tottering ruins and romantic hovels without heeding the rottenness and squalor of the place. In the false haven of a highly coloured pamphlet, the fascination of the East does not seem so very distant, yet on every side is evidence of putrescence and decay.

The transference of the capital to Ankara and the collapse of the Sultan's court and the Caliphate has removed some, at least, of the exotic veneer. For the rest, I think the abandonment of Mohammedanism by the bulk of the population is perhaps the most important. The westernisation of costume has deprived it of a great deal of the colour, and certainly the boycott of the yashmak destroyed the mystery.

The contrast between the monuments of Constantinople as described by history and imagination, and their shabby remains, is at first peculiar and sickening. The air of devastation and disaster hangs heavy. Degradation and death proclaim, not alone from the multitude of decrepit graveyards within the boundary walls, but from the crumbling remnants of this ancient bulwark of Christian civilisation. The dregs and debris of the modern city cover it like a cloying veil, concealing and burying that older Byzantine city on which it has lain for nearly five centuries.

To the north-west of Karieh Djami, within an acre of scarred and desolated landscape, is a foul, repulsive ruin. Its thick walls of brick and marble are of sixth-century workmanship. On the north, beneath the vacant windows, a few mangy horses eke out a miserable and famished existence. From here is the only entrance. One clambers over great heaps of filth, and large, bloated rats scurry across one's path. The floors have fallen centuries ago. In the centre three dead horses lie bloody and unburied, half eaten away. No spot can be more repellent. It is a wing of the far famed Palace of Justinian. From here he issued every Sunday, wearing his Imperial robes and attended by all the pomp and ceremony of the Byzantine Emperor, to attend divine service at the Cathedral of Sancta Sophia. The rooms of the palace were separated by doors of silver. They were furnished with incredible wealth and extravagance. The floor of the bedroom of the Empress has been described as a meadow sparkling with jewels. There was the Iris Room, with its stalactite ceiling, a predecessor of the room in the Turkish seraglio ; and the Banqueting Hall with its silver candelabra, its nineteen ivory tables and gold plate sufficient for two hundred and twenty-nine guests ; and above all, the Throne Room where the Emperor reigned as the Lord's Anointed and Representative of the Son of God. Now all is past, and as one looks out from these empty windows over the sordid grounds it is very difficult to imagine that here were once pavilions and terraces and fountains of rose water.

CONSTANTINOPLE.

Very little of the actual city of Constantine survives. Earthquakes and fires, the repeated sieges of the city and the brutal destructions which followed its capture by the Crusaders and the Ottoman Turks, have all combined to make it extremely difficult to find any of the original superstructure. But of the substructure, the city preserves its original reservoirs. These great cisterns were filled from mammoth aqueducts, Roman in design and construction, which spanned the city with Brobdignagian arches. These could, however, only furnish a variable, and in times of drought ann isufficient, supply ; in war-time even that might be intercepted. So they created this elaborate system of reservoirs, one to each hill. Of these cisterns the greatest was the first, and was constructed by Philoxemos, a Senator who came from Rome with Constantine.

The entrance is rather insignificant, just off a main street quite close to Sancta Sophia. It leads down a rather dark and dingy corridor to a kiosk where admission tickets and photographs are for sale. From there a guide leads the way, and our footsteps echo rather uncannily. He has large rubber boots which give deep reverberating thuds, while my shoes echo staccato, like pistol shots. It is almost impossible to see and I have to feel my way along the damp walls. We are going downhill all the way, till we reach some sort of a wooden platform and the guide leaves me with a warning to stay where I am. I can hear a peculiar tinkling noise, like the falling of thin metal leaves through space. It is still and cold and now absolutely dark, till suddenly the guide, only a few feet away, switches on a few pinpoint lights which dimly illuminate a seemingly endless procession of columns rising out of lacquer-black water, the whole effect crushing in its vague immensity and by the sense of overwhelming space. This cistern is now called Bin Bir Derek, or The Thousand and One Columns ; each column is inscribed with the name of its patrician donor, so it comes to us to-day as a very monumental and princely Roll of Honour.

We get into a tiny rowing boat and start to explore the darkness. The thing which impresses one most about this journey is its strange sense of unreality. Rowing over water so completely dark and undisturbed is like gliding on black polished rubber, a feeling which is enhanced by the skill of the guide as he lets the oars penetrate the surface without a splash or ripple.

How long we travelled I do not know. It was as though we were on some eternal plane in which time and space had ceased to have any relation with human faculties, but was composed of certain geometric forms which repeated themselves in a changeless monotony.

CONSTANTINOPLE.

The churches of Constantinople, transformed to mosques, come down to us hallowed by the memory of unutterable misfortune. There is squalor and decay about so much of the architecture of Constantinople, that one cannot help feeling the depression is due not so much to its present ruinous state as to the air of apathy and neglect which pervades the city. Even the face of a city destroyed by earthquake or war would not, I imagine, exude the same dreadful sense of hopelessness a ndof incurability ; and it is in the churches that one cannot help noticing this most. The virtual abolition of Mohammedanism in Turkey has left the smaller mosques empty and unattended ; and these mosques were once Christian churches.

This picture may at first seem a rather depressing one, but there is the real hope that the Government will some day, and I trust it may be soon, take steps to restore at least the most noteworthy. For these churches, in a condition at present that would discredit an urban refuse dump, contain the whole clue to the history of art from Roman to Mediæval and Renaissance times. It stirs up a feeling of despondency to see them falling into decay while the great conglomeration of buildings which forms the Palace of the Sultans is treated with absurd reverence and carefully preserved as a focal point for the tourists.

The condition of the Church of Christ Pantocrator is typical of many. It was built at the command of the Empress Eirene, and consists of three parallel but unequal churches, separated only by colonnades and all entered from the same imposing narthex. On the south is the main cathedral ; on the north the monastic church, and in the centre a smaller church which served as a mausoleum. The first to lie there was Eirene, the foundress. Later it was filled with the tombs of succeeding monarchs, but to-day the vaults of the Imperial dead are inhabited by Turkish households, not dead but living, or, should I say, barely existing. In these surroundings they lodge amid indescribable filth and squalor. It seems incredible that this church was once praised for the surpassing beauty of its mosaiced interior, which was inlaid by " the most cunning artists " ; and these mosaics, almost certainly there as at Sancta Sophia, are only awaiting the removal of the plaster which covers them.

I am not proposing to enumerate all the churches of Constantinople. Here and there one is compensated by fragments of art and architecture of great beauty and significance. But the visitor has to have such enthusiasm for the historical and the beautiful that he is encouraged to persist even when he finds the scantiest scraps which possess these characteristics. The churches stand to-day where no account is taken of these things. They have been in the charge of infidels who have little or no appreciation of their beauty ; whose sense of art is limited to the whitewash brush and crude repetitive stencilling. This form of decoration is typical of Mohammedan art at its worst, and suggests the atmosphere of a boarding-house lavatory rather than a House of God.

After saying so much in depreciation of the present city as I see it to-day, it would be grossly unfair if I did not mention the great mosques of Istanbul which give it on

111

S. MARY PAMMAKARISTOS, CONSTANTINOPLE

CHRIST PANTOCRATOR, CONSTANTINOPLE

H

arrival that extraordinary illusion of a Celestial City. The legacy of Byzantine architecture proved to be a source of inspiration for the Turkish builders in their endeavour to emulate the Christian style. The evolution from the simple domed structure to the multi-domed Mosque of Sultan Ahmet is continuous, and brings to a conclusion the sequence of architectural development.

The mosques are the noblest monuments of the Ottoman Empire and of a religion which is as fast disappearing in Turkey as the power of Kemal Pasha grows. With a care they never expended on the palaces and kiosks of the Seraglio, and an art which found its greatest stimulus in Sancta Sophia, they endeavoured to create their mosques as splendid and permanent as man could devise and construct.

The Mosque of Sultan Ahmet and Sancta Sophia stand facing each other at either end of the ancient Hippodrome, the one the supreme endeavour of the Christian, the other of the Ottoman. Within the mosque four columns, seventy feet in circumference, each encased in exquisite Persian tiles, carry the dome fifteen feet higher than Sancta Sophia. Both possess the same feeling of spaciousness and grandeur and monumental scale; both are the consecration of their highest art in the service of their Faith; both emphasise the sublimity of the heavens and the insignificance of man. But the difference is vast. Their likeness is only that of the fresh pea and the canned; one of form and line, construction and size. The mosques have a cold, almost deathlike air, whereas what thrills one so much in Sancta Sophia is the warmth of feeling and spacious atmospheric glow which fills the entire church.

I remember once seeing an exhibition of pictures of the London scene by a young Japanese artist. The depiction was as truthful photographically as he could make it; and yet the result was completely foreign. The colour seemed brighter, more vivid, and the atmosphere clearer and purer. Even a London fog had a mystic Eastern air as it writhed over St. James's Park where the artist found the inevitable willow tree dripping its branches into an evidently Oriental pool. His translation of the English Metropolis was as different from the London of the Cockney as the Mosque of Sultan Ahmet from the Church of Sancta Sophia.

The Ottoman followed the constructional ideas of the Byzantine to its ultimate conclusion, but never achieved the greatness of Sancta Sophia, which is vastness and simplicity itself. Day after day I returned there to watch the sun's rays penetrate the circumference of the dome and pass over every detail, contemplating the splendours in mysterious limelight till they dissolved into a vague obscurity in the evening and the magic silence of the empty church was broken by the tinkling of a bell and the Turkish equivalent of " Time, gentlemen, please." Each day I reluctantly followed the guide's steps and was shut out with the clanking of the gate; till the last day came and the mind was filled only with the memories of that most daring, most poetic, creation of architecture.

The time has passed too quickly and one recollects many vivid, precious moments, even if at times it has seemed difficult to penetrate the Moslem veil which enshrouds the city.

The steamer cuts the waves of Marmora and I look back with regret into the ever-increasing gloom to see Sancta Sophia, Church of Holy Wisdom, marked by four stately minarets, a fast fading silhouette.

MOSQUE OF SULTAN AHMET, CONSTANTINOPLE 115

CHAPTER SIX

THE STORY OF THE BYZANTINE EMPIRE, AFTER THE
fall of Constantinople to the Knights of the Fourth Crusade, is
filled with romance and tragedy. The Imperial exiles established their court first at Nicea, then at Trebizond, and finally at
Mistra in the Morea.

At Nicea the Emperor Michael Paleologus conspired to over-
throw the Latin conquerors ; there the patriots plotted and
planned the re-conquest of Constantinople ; and the Cæsars of
New Rome lived in a temporary haven, creating for a time an
image of the glory and traditions of the Empire. From Constantinople the Senate, princes and artists fled to these new cities
and the culture of the age was preserved.

When the Crusaders, after diverting from their original
intention of saving the Holy Land from the Infidels, sailed for
Constantinople, Geoffrey Villehardouin was waiting for them with a large force at
a port in Palestine. Deciding not to be left out of the inevitable plunder, he set out to
join his friends. Unfortunately his ships were driven off their route by storms and he
was forced to land at Modon on the south-west of the Morea.

Up till the Frankish conquest the Government of the Morea by the Byzantines had
been purely nominal, and the control lay in the charge of a few wealthy families, none
too friendly with each other. It was a simple accomplishment for Villehardouin to
capture the Morea and establish at Mistra his capital. In 1245 he was succeeded by his
brother William, who got into trouble with Michael Paleologus, the Pretender to the
throne of Byzantium. William was captured and compelled to surrender the greater
portion of the Morea. In 1259 Michael regained the Imperial Crown, and three years
later Mistra became the residence of Constantine, his brother, and was eventually raised
to the status of despotate. The despots of Mistra, exerting absolute power within their
provinces, were, however, allied to the Empire, by whose ambassadors they were
represented abroad.

For two hundred years Mistra prospered and attained considerable eminence as a seat
of culture and learning. But there was ever present the menace of the Turks, who,
driven from behind by the Mongol invasion, lay scattered in nomadic disorder throughout
Asia Minor. In 1306 they crossed to Europe ; in 1385 Sophia was captured, in 1430
Salonika, and twenty-three years later, after a siege of fifty-three days, the Turks entered
Constantinople. Still the Empire persevered at Mistra and Trebizond. The latter fell
in 1461, leaving only Mistra. There the brothers of the last Constantine maintained to
the bitter end the traditions of the Empire, re-establishing to some extent the glories of
the capital. But for the Turks, Mistra might have continued to prosper for centuries.
The fatal year 1462 marked the close of the Byzantine Empire and the end of Greek
dominion in Europe ; an end of that brief period which alone relieves the failure of

Greek mediæval art. Greece as a country had done little in the promotion of Christian art. This last great epoch might have been particularly her own, if only Fate had spared her the intolerance of Ottoman tyranny. The evidence at Mistra indicates a Byzantine Renaissance which might have surpassed all that had gone before, and one which is only now being fully recognised.

The fashion of historians to divide the subject of their studies into periods of Rise, Decline and Fall, has become so habitual that it would seem to be almost inevitable that a fall should succeed an apparent decline. We know that on several historic occasions a civilisation has degenerated and the fall has been quite clearly defined ; but it would be wrong, for the sake of finality and uniformity of order, to assume that the three phases must be passed through. Contemporary research has shown that at the time of the annexation of the Empire by the Turks, Byzantine art and culture had reached a point never exceeded. The mosaics of Karieh Djami have already been described. The paintings of Mistra are of the same period. The art which had for so long been restrained by the dogmas of the Church had at long last entered a freer, more humanistic, phase.

The city of Mistra, scattered over the slopes of a rocky outcrop of the Tagetus range, some 2,000 feet above sea level and two and a half miles from ancient Sparta, is the only city which truly evokes the spirit of Byzantine secular life. It was still inhabited at the beginning of the nineteenth century and has only lately been recognised as the most remarkable ruined city in Europe. Unlike ancient Pompeii, where every fresco and mosaiced floor is railed off in the fashion of an alfresco museum, Mistra has an authentic and unadulterated air. At Pompeii it was with considerable effort that one restored to memory the long gone ghosts from history books. Here is present—reality. One feels that real people walked and shopped in these narrow lanes which lead upward to the Palace of the Despots and further to the massive walls of the castle of William Villehardouin, Prince of Achaia.

The present desolation of Mistra is at first a part of its charm, but later its misfortune. It is pleasant to climb the narrow streets, free to look at and study what one pleases without being bothered with constant interruptions of guides or tourists. In these last few days I have been the sole visitor to Mistra, only meeting occasionally one of the six black-robed inhabitants of the Pantanassa, a convent, high above all the other churches at Mistra in merit and situation. These lively old ladies are the only inhabitants of the city, and it is thanks to their care that such of the frescoes as remain are preserved ; for the churches are falling sadly to ruin. With the single exception of the Pantanassa, all are rotting with damp. The Church of the Brontocheion has been intentionally demolished, in part, for lack of building material to restore the more venerable Church of S. Demetrius. Now its frescoes are open to all the elements. The oil lamps, placed below the frescoes with such loving care by the nuns, are sadly inefficient deterrents to mildew. But better typewriters than mine have already stamped out enraged sentences at this major tragedy.

MISTRA.

The Metropolitan Church of S. Demetrius is situated at the foot of the town and contains the earliest paintings of Mistra. These, dating back to the beginning of the fourteenth century, before Mistra was a capital city, follow old conventions and are therefore clearly isolated from the Byzantine Renaissance so conspicuous elsewhere in the city. It was here, in 1453, that Constantine XI, the last of the eighty-eight Emperors of Constantinople, was crowned King and Emperor of New Rome. A stone carved with the Imperial Eagles marks the spot. This coat of arms of the double-headed eagle, which looks east and west over Asia and Europe, was to be adopted thirty-five years later by Ivan III of Russia; and in 1547 his grandson, surnamed the Terrible, raised the Eagle of the Third Rome, claiming for himself the title of Tsar or Cæsar, justifying his elevated rank by direct descent from Vladimir, son-in-law of the Emperor Constantine IX. In doing this Ivan the Terrible assumed a title which carried not only temporal but divine power; and a title which was maintained with all its significance up to the Russian Revolution, and was recognised by the whole Slavonic world.

The part played by Russia in the development of Byzantine art begins at Kiev, in the tenth century, where Greek artists were invited to assist in the construction and decoration of her new churches. But it was not until the reign of Ivan the Terrible that orthodoxy triumphed over Islam. From that time there still endures one memorial, the most fantastic creation in Europe, the Church of S. Basil, the Vassili Blagennoi, in the Red Square at Moscow. It was built then and the conquered city of Kazan paid for its erection. It expresses in a sort of barbaric grandeur a great deal of the Byzantine spirit. The continued existence of Byzantine culture after the fall of Constantinople is proof of its remarkable vitality. The art of Rumania witnessed at Voronet and Sucavita

S. DEMETRIUS, MISTRA

an artistic revival of purely Byzantine origin long after the collapse of that Christian Empire. At Meteora, and more particularly Mount Athos, this culture has survived to the present century, and there seems to be little reason to believe that it will not continue to endure.

MISTRA.

It is a remarkable thing that, while painting was tending towards Renaissance, the art of sculpture of this period showed no similar development ; all the more remarkable when we consider that this Renaissance was paralleled in thought and culture through the direct influence of a school of philosophy at Mistra which followed the inspiration and teachings of Plato. For it seems reasonable to assume that there should be a tendency towards the heroic idealism of classic sculpture. But we find none of that.

The aversion to anything akin to naturalistic representation of the human form seems to have been carried at Mistra to its ultimate conclusion. We find, instead of subtle form, that the Oriental tendency to pattern in low relief has at last become little more than engraving on stone. It cannot truthfully be classed as sculpture any more ; the only resemblance is in the material of its execution. But if results of this sort cannot be termed sculpture, they can still remain works of art, and works of real importance in the history of Byzantine art.

The seated Christ in the Metropolis at Mistra is perhaps the finest example we have of this last phase. There is no attempt at natural expression. The figure of Christ is raised a couple of inches in front of the background. On this silhouetted form, drapery and features are suggested simply by incised lines. The background is profusely decorated in interlacing pattern, and there is indication that this was originally covered with gold leaf and colour. This last must have removed any pretence to sculpture, while making it all the more interesting as pure pattern on stone. The simplicity and directness of expression is the feature that appeals and is most characteristic.

It must be remembered that the artist's aim was the representation of the Divine in the way that would be most easily understood, avoiding at all costs any representation that would encourage in the mind of the spectator thought of earthly things. It is essential that this is understood before attempting any criticism of Byzantine art. I have already said that Art for Art's Sake seems to me a particularly misleading phrase ; art has a purpose, and the best art is the best expression of that purpose. The art of the Byzantines was never naturalistic, even in its last and newest phase of painting ; its main purpose was not to please, but was essentially an endeavour to depict as clearly as possible the spiritual faith of their times.

MISTRA.

The frescoes of Pantanassa should rank exceedingly high in any list of the world's masterpieces. They are certainly the finest examples that remain of the art of the Byzantines. Unlike Mr. Huxley, who dared to assess the Resurrection, by Piero della Francesca, at San Sepolcro, as the finest picture in the world, I have neither the courage nor the authority to determine the true æsthetic status of the wall paintings of Pantanassa.

CHRIST, MISTRA   121

122   FRESCOES, PANTANASSA, MISTRA

But I am prepared to say that these paintings display a quality in art unsurpassed by anything I have yet seen.

This art shows a new and exciting development from the almost stereotyped forms of the earlier Byzantine ; we find traditional subjects filled with new characters and material and at times we discover entire new scenes. The scheme of colour is more comprehensive and the technique is found, upon examination, to have anticipated the French Impressionists by three hundred years. The calculated method of placing contrasting colours in immediate proximity to each other, so that a particularly vivid compound is visible from the right distance, is seen at Pantanassa in its earliest and most vivid stages. Colours are used more and more for the pattern and design they achieve. The paintings have no longer a staid tranquillity, but have an emotional and picturesque significance that can only be paralleled in present artistic achievement.

MISTRA.

The immigrations of diverse architectural styles are among the most remarkable and regrettable features of recent English industrial and cosmopolitan life. Within a century the English countryside has been filled with an astonishing hotch-potch of synthetic design. And yet this vagrant habit of constructional and superficial details was, until the industrial era, entirely salutary. It produced every masterpiece of Gothic and Renaissance, while at the same time evolving unmistakable English characteristics. It is this power of facile adaptation which, up to a point, distinguishes great epochs. But in the last century the English did not adapt but adopt ; they copied details wholesale, irrespective of merit or suitability, with remarkably little discrimination or judgment.

The Byzantine epoch drew inspiration from the remotest outskirts of the empire to create a culture which spread throughout the civilised world. Byzantine architecture, which is the concrete expression of its culture, is not essentially Greek, essentially Roman or essentially Eastern, but a careful fusion of all three.

Even in its last impoverished phase, the architecture which had so long been true to its triple pedigree was not completely conservative. With the arrival of Geoffrey Villehardouin, ideas were brought from France which found their place in the new church of Pantanassa. The bell tower, with its trefoiled arches, can be identified with those in Aquitaine. All this is fairly obvious, but the really remarkable feature is that we see at Pantanassa details of architecture which, after originating at Constantinople and passing to Aquitaine, return here modified after five hundred years, to be adapted anew by their originators. The similarity of Pantanassa to the churches in Aquitaine has already been remarked by others. On a larger scale, and in the same district, the cathedral of Perigueux is essentially the same as S. Mark's, Venice, and its prototype, the Church of the Twelve Apostles, Constantinople.

MISTRA.

It would be wrong, even at the risk of monotony, to make no mention of the Church of Peribleptos, at the farthest end of the twisting narrow lane from Pantanassa. My ambition to record the Byzantine legacy in Greece, though in the light of its vast quantity

PANTANASSA, MISTRA

PERIBLEPTOS, MISTRA

proved impossible in entirety, makes it imperative that I do not fail as the occasion arises to add the more notable to this present store.

Most Byzantine churches are isolated units, set on a site apart. This, indeed, is typical. Other buildings may be set closely around the church, as in the monasteries of Mount Athos, but seldom, if ever, come into immediate contact with it. This isolation is not usual in the monasteries of Western Europe, where we find great cloisters connecting directly the church and the monastic buildings. But the Byzantine church is generally a complete unit which one can walk around and study from all angles ; except at Peribleptos, where we find our viewpoint strictly limited, for the western end is hollowed out of the cliff face and the east is somewhat confused by subsidiary building at a lower level. Entrance is obtained from the side. The church is of the two-column variety, the dome being carried on two columns on the west and two piers on the east. These piers are prolonged to form the central apse. Once more we find elements received from the west, a fleur-de-lis and rosettes carved on the face of the apse, and once more we find frescoes of considerable charm, yet again suffering from damp and decay. Some of the vacant windows have been boarded up as a means of protection from the weather, so that the place seems rather dark and dingy, and to see the frescoes, candles have to be obtained.

But when all is said, Mistra is incomparably lovely. I stayed here much longer than I had intended. One simply does not want to leave. Each day from Sparta I have returned, till a brief note from the bank makes it imperative that this tour be protracted no longer ; so I looked for the last time across the Lacedæmonian Plain, over the new sown fields and the olive groves, and yet nearer, over the rich tiled roofs of the scattered remains of Mistra.

From the nuns I received my last cup of coffee, the last of many. It was goodbye, and eight o'clock.

CRISSAFA.

The distance from Sparta to Crissafa is about eleven kilometres, and eight of these are uphill. But the effort is well repaid, for Crissafa possesses not only a charming church but a charming host in Father Sava, who presides there every Sunday. It also possesses an American Greek, an unfortunate but inevitable character in every village. He speaks a singular tongue which recalls to mind the gangster films of one's youth. His story is typical of most ; the Tough Guy Makes Good. He describes at length the history of his accumulated fortune which makes it possible for him to retire while his fellows, who know no better, will probably work here all their days. Yes, *sir*. And having got that off his chest, he wants to know if I am an American, and if I know Pottsville, Pa. It seems that Pottsville is a swell town and that I ought to know it. He figures that it is strange to visit Greece when one could make a fortune in Pottsville, Pa. It sure is, buddy, he says. You make a big mistake. . . . Nothing here. . . . Nope. . . . Not a dime. I mention the purpose of my visit. Churches ? Say, that's only stones. Yes, *sir*. Just a heap of stones.

It would be useless to point out to him that these stones are so cunningly constructed that they have preserved for centuries one of the most remarkable and complete cycles of Byzantine mural decoration I have ever seen. Remarkable because, unlike Mistra, though of the same date, they are absolutely intact.

Technically, the great bulk of Byzantine wall decoration is not fresco, but tempera painting. In fresco the plaster is not allowed to dry before the colours are applied, and these are compounded with lime so that they adhere absolutely and in fact become one with the plaster when set. But you have to work fast and cannot correct your mistakes. Tempera painting, on the other hand, is applied when the plaster is dry, and the colours have been mixed with some adhesive medium, such as white of egg or size. The result has not, of course, the same degree of permanency, as the colours are liable to flake off through the deterioration of the adhesive.

The procedure of painting in tempera was always the same. First the drawing was carried out in lines of red, and colours were applied by superimposed coats till the required depth of tone was reached. Then shading was applied in lines of brown or black and the high lights picked out last by pure white lines.

This technique is clearly apparent at Crissafa, where by some unfortunate chance all the blues and greens have faded to white, leaving there only the lines of construction. At first the effect is rather strange, almost monochromatic, having the quality of a sepia photograph or a painting limited to a palette of reds and browns. Where the colour has faded the drawing is clear, and particularly in the representation of Christ's robe, every tentative line made by the artist is discovered. It is rather strange to see a painting which was complete four hundred years ago and is now partially revealed in the stage of original sketch. Interesting, too, to note in this last period the absence of symbolism and the clear depiction of the subject which makes it no longer necessary to add the customary descriptive texts.

AGIOI SARANTA.

It is eight kilometres from Crissafa to Agioi Saranta; eight kilometres of forlorn dusty road stretching between low desolate hillsides, forming wild narrow valleys with here and there a few bare, windy trees somehow attached to the landscape but not a part of it. They are the merest incidents along the road. The earth must have looked like this before the coming of man. It is primeval, far, far more impressive than scenic beauty. And after these eight kilometres Agioi Saranta is reached.

Agioi Saranta is a monastery not unlike the monasteries of Athos, but covered thick with layer upon layer of whitewash so that the corners are softened and the bricks no longer clear; it is still essentially the same. The great stretches of galleried living quarters, the refectory, the church and the phiale are all in their respective places. Only the massive arsenal, or guardian tower, is absent from the now familiar composition. Outside, a second church, smaller but fundamentally the same in construction and design, is built on a hummock overlooking the monastery. This church, for some reason, seems more attractive than its parent; perhaps because of its smallness.

The fascination of the model and the minute is a strange part of the mind's composition, one that persists from childhood days. While the young female of the species

AGIOI SARANTA, PELOPONNESUS
Opposite: FRESCOES, CRISSAFA

I

Above: S. DEMETRIUS, MISTRA
Below: THE ROCK OF MONAMVASIA

is immersed in dolls houses and shops of tiny dimensions, her male counterpart creates toy theatres, plays with diminutive soldiers and makes model airplanes. Always it is smaller editions of the real thing which seem to enchant. To be fascinated by the miniature is, I think, a typical reaction of most people, and I cannot help feeling it is perhaps a part of the attraction of Byzantine architecture in its latest stage. The buildings are all so tiny and yet so perfectly proportioned. They are not of great consequence in architectural history, but they are attractive. They do not inspire and impress like Sancta Sophia, but fascinate as only small things can. But however small the little church of Agioi Saranta is, it still maintains all the characteristics of good design and sensitive craftsmanship which originated at Constantinople, and of which Greece ultimately was the natural inheritor.

MONAMVASIA.

Travelling by bus in Greece is always an adventure, and one which starts long before the bus. The persistent cramming of people, luggage and livestock into the strictly limited capacity of the bus disproves the theory that you can't put a quart into a pint pot. In just the same way, before I left London, five roomsful of furniture were somehow packed into a tiny van that could have been garaged in my bathroom.

Movement of any sort was impossible. Half a dozen hens, each having one ankle tied to its neighbour, perched on the rack above my head, to my recurrent dismay. A prime pig snorted his disgust from the luggage grid at the back. But at last we were off, to the cheers of the Spartan crowd, and settled with every bump more and more securely into the wedge of luggage and sweating humanity. So we jogged on to Monamvasia, where I was prized out and presented by my neighbour, the proud owner of the hens, with a couple of eggs.

" You can't get them fresher than that," he said in effect, as he lifted them off the rack.

MONAMVASIA.

Monamvasia has all the attraction of the spectacular and the fantastic. Situated on a mammoth rock, just off the coast of Maleas, fifty miles south of Sparta, it is not unlike Mont S. Michel. It is attached to the mainland in much the same way by a narrow finger of road, which leads to the steep terraced town and ultimately the cathedral at the summit.

The rock is about a mile long and six hundred feet in height. This natural stronghold was the last to fall to the Franks, and with Mistra it returned to Byzantine dominion ; later it fell to the Turks with the rest of the Morea, and for a brief interlude at the end of the seventeenth century it was governed from Venice.

The town itself is a vivid little place, terraced on the rockside down to the sea. Above are vineyards and olives and gigantic cacti. Then bare rock to the citadel, where the cathedral Church of S. Sophia decays amidst the ruins of the military town. From the top, the flat roofs below look like some Giant's Causeway, stepping up the rockside out of the sea to the red scarred cliffs close at hand. And in the distance the flattened hills of Maleas roll out to the furthest horizon.

S. SOPHIA, MONAMVASIA

Back to the town, where the Church of S. Nicholas, with its curious Renaissance doorway, a product of the Venetian occupation, is the centre of interest. This church is remarkable as an expression of sheer structural form, in which the doorway has no real significance but seems to prefix the main building in deference to the Venetian conquerors; for it was built during the Venetian occupation, as an inscription confirms. Its walls, strong and forbidding, are grey, smeared with white, sympathetic only to the cragged coast. There is no patterning of brickwork or richly tiled roof here. Instead, we find an architecture reduced to bare essentials, severely expressing structure alone.

MONAMVASIA.

> This is a story, somewhat drear,
> Of Clarence, Duke and Royal Peer,
> Whose death occurred, I must relate,
> In Year of Grace, One Four Seven Eight.
> He met his fate, not on a line,
> But in a butt of Malmsey Wine.

Malmsey, a product of Monamvasia, is a rather sweet, aromatic wine, not to be confused with Malvoisie, the Frankish imitation. The curious historic episode of the drowning of the Duke of Clarence has thus a certain significance in this present soliloquy. Connections between England and anything Byzantine are scarce. The death of an English duke in Byzantine wine is a rare occasion. Before this, however, in the year 1400 to be precise, the Byzantine Emperor Manuel solicited aid from Henry IV of England to save the Empire from the Turks. He was received with the honour and respect due to an emperor, but unfortunately no assistance was given. This immediate danger was, however, averted, as the Turks at that time were attacked in the rear by the great Tamerlaine.

ARGOS.

I left Monamvasia in the early morning, again bumping and rattling over that same mud track road, my eyes straining through the golden opacity of celluloid at the back of the bus to see for the last time the great outline of the rock. Sad now at the parting, for this Grecian episode is drawing to a close. All too soon I must leave Greece. But for the present there are the interminable hills, reddened in the sun, and the almond and peach trees, covering their lowest slopes with blossom, pinky white. At Allivi we stop for coffee, but no longer. I take a snapshot of the church, just off the road, clean and white in the morning sun, but have not time to get inside or learn its history. It looks very lovely—but the bus is waiting. Impatiently the horn toots, I scramble in and off we go. Reaching Sparta, we start to climb, and from a vantage point get just a glimpse of Mistra, sprawling indistinctly brown below Villehardouin's castle on an insignificant foothill of Tagetus; then up and over the highest hills along the twisting narrow ribbon of road until we come to the wide valley and to Argos at its centre. This is the first stage back.

S. NICHOLAS, MONAMVASIA

S. NICHOLAS, MONAMVASIA

ALLIVI, PELOPONNESUS

ATHENS.

This morning, the last but one, was very cold and sunny; later, in a hermetically sealed railway carriage, very hot and stuffy. The train ran easily, arriving in Corinth remarkably close to schedule. It passed across the great cliffs of the canal, along by the sea, above the sea, gently undulating and twisting up and down and swinging along to Athens.

Returning to Athens is like coming home from school. Friends have to be visited, one's every adventure described at great length. I told them of an escapade with Percy, the mule, so called because it rhymed with its name in Greek. We were alone in the mountains and Percy, after refusing to budge for some time, suddenly remembered something, scampered over the hills and far away. Within a minute he was over the horizon, beyond sight. I don't know how many hours I searched for the beast, but it was quite dark when I returned to Sparta and the owner, a sadder but not much wiser man.

But the owner had an idea. We walked across the yard to the stable and there was Percy, having extricated himself from my luggage, now chewing my last cake of chocolate, paper and all. After detailing this story once or twice I began to wonder, though it seemed to amuse, if it was really funny at all. It certainly wasn't at the time.

Lastly there are the handshakes, the farewells, the interminable goodbyes. Must I really go? Just so soon? Didn't I want to stay? There was so much more I ought to see.

Oh, yes, I knew that so well, if only I could. This trip has shown so little, and there is so much. But it is all settled now; the cabin is booked, the ship at anchor, and tourist lire in my pocket.

EN ROUTE.

Now that it's passed, I sit on deck remembering only the beauty and the pleasure of these last months. The inevitable incidents, the exhausted patience with the lethargic Greek, the constant struggle for lebensraum in bedrooms overcrowded by insect life, all these recede and are forgotten. From the upper deck, over the waters I see near at hand the Eleusian Plain, and in the distance the clouds standing high upon Parnassus. There is a beauty in Greece beyond compare, something quite distinct from Constantinople. Here is the beauty of a living thing, not the pathetic vacuity of a Turkish museum; for Constantinople bears too strongly the impress of the conquerors, while Greece maintains without a break the tradition of centuries.

The steamer drives on towards the sun, the undulating line of mountains sink lower and lower till they fall and are lost beneath the horizon's rim. But next morning the even perimeter of sea is broken again, now by the Italian coast, and from there gulls fly towards us, greet their Greek brethren and swoop down alongside to accompany us over the remaining stretch. And I turn yet one more page of the International Phrase Book.

137

BRINDISI IS A PLEASANT ENOUGH PLACE, and must be almost unique in a country so packed with holiday haunts and show places. There is the Church of Santa Lucia which preserves, in the crypt, a remarkable frescoed Virgin and Child of the twelfth century, and there is the colossal Corinthian column marking the terminus of the Appian Way. But that seems to be all, and there only remain the long avenue of trees down the main street, the cafés and the proscenium of gigantic palms before the ships with brightly coloured sails dancing in the harbour. However, it's all very pleasant. It almost seems that Brindisi is attractive because it has so few attractions.

The significance of Italy, and more particularly Rome, as a centre of early Christianity and culture, is recognised, but the full importance of the Greek influence in Italy has not yet been sufficiently appreciated. The art of Rome was essentially imitative. It developed from the cultures of Egypt and Greece a monumental art on an imperial scale, but basically it created nothing that was new. In Rome there was always a large Greek colony, a colony which was among the first to accept the Christian faith. Naples was a Greek city and latterly, in the south and in Sicily, the preponderance of Greeks was such that the Athenian idiom has persisted up till quite recent times.

All round the heel and toe of Italy Greek monks had settled, instituting monasteries or living as solitaries in rugged eyries cut into the hillsides. In the sixth century their number was augmented by the arrival of Syrian ascetics driven by the Saracens from Egypt and the northern shores of Africa. Then, at the time of the iconoclast persecution, some 50,000 refugees fled here and found themselves quite at home in a country that was already Byzantine. These people continued to recognise the Patriarch at Constantinople in preference to the Pope; and for so long as Rome was weakened by the pagan incursions of Goths and Vandals she was compelled to suffer the ritual of the Eastern Church. It was not till the thirteenth century that, with the growth of power in the West and the temporary fall of Constantinople in the East, the Roman system supplanted the Byzantine.

South Italy retains little of the Byzantine period. There is a number of the rock-cut hermitages frescoed in the traditional manner, the ruined monastery of S. Angelo di Raparo, and one or two Byzantine churches. But all exemplify in their art that extraordinarily beautiful combination of Syrian and Greek, Orient and Occident, which is called Byzantine, and which is seen to advantage at Brindisi in the crypt of Santa Lucia.

From the eleventh century the south of Italy was governed along with Sicily by Norman Kings. It is not commonly appreciated that the Norman Conquest covered a considerable area in addition to England. The achievement of 1066 was only a part of a much wider scheme. Early in the century the Normans had established themselves in Italy, and in 1038 went to the assistance of the Byzantines in an endeavour to drive the Saracens out of Sicily, but three years later captured the country for themselves. Under the Norman kingship, art in Southern Italy, and more especially in Sicily, developed the inheritance of Byzantine and Saracen. Of this period in Italy there remains the Church of SS. Nicola and Cataldo, at Lecce, twenty miles south of Brindisi.

LECCE.

The train south followed the coast, but hedged in as it was by enormous candelabra of cactus, one saw remarkably little sea. Every now and then the train would stop at villages to pick up occasional passengers. Each village, composed of little white cubes of uniform size and punctuated with dots of windows, is scattered over the plain like the cast of gigantic dice.

The Church of S. Cataldo was a disappointment. Though it was built in 1180, it retains remarkably little of that period ; a couple of doors, one in the middle of a wretched Baroque façade and the other in the cloister, both engraved with Byzantine and Saracen motives, were all there was to see.

Later, in the town, Saint Cataldo, in the form of a highly coloured statue, was being taken for his birthday airing. Up and down the town, by four crimson robed pall-bearers and a number of monks and novices following in procession. To complete the show, a brass band trumpeted its way along as a sort of rearguard, while at the sides the lay brothers were collecting the donations of the sightseers in little black bags. It reminded me of Students' Day in Edinburgh, when we marched in fancy dress, collecting pennies for the Infirmary. At Lecce, this religious ceremony seemed somehow to have assumed a similar character of masquerade. To the Byzantine, this public exhibitionism, this blatant propaganda, would seem nauseatingly irreverent. There each man must carry his own torch to light the way along the mysterious Orthodox path ; but here the efficient clergy of the Roman Church mark their way with a blaze of rosy lights.

ROSSANO.

It is curious that the documentary evidence of early Christianity should be so slight, and that not one of the original manuscripts of the Gospels exists. The fact is that there is no authentic Christian literature preserved that is earlier than the fourth century A.D., and only two documents have been discovered of that period, the Codex Sinaiticus and the Codex Vaticanus. Both are written in Greek, the language of most Christians of the Roman Empire. The earliest portable literature was inscribed on long papyrus rolls, and it is presumed that the original Gospels must have taken this form. One roll could not have contained more than one Gospel, but the Codices, or the first paged books, included generally the four Gospels in one volume and the Pauline Epistles in another. In the centuries that followed, book production made great progress, and it became quite fashionable in early Byzantine times to possess a book, as it was in our father's day to own a library. By the fifth century, books became a vehicle not only for literature but for illustration. They were richly illuminated, and in themselves became works of art. The Codex Rossanensis and the Vienna Genesis are the supreme examples of fifth-century workmanship. The former, the object of this present visit, is superb. Inscribed in silver characters on a deep and royal purple vellum, with illustrations that have a richness and a variety of colour and of design, it seems a remarkable production for a period which was so austere and so conservative in its artistic sensibility. It does in fact precede chronologically all we have yet seen, and seems to set the fashion for the art of the Byzantines some three hundred years later. And yet, when one comes to think of it, this is not so very surprising ; for after all the work of the illuminator was a comparatively private affair and was not tied, as was that of the mural decorator and mosaic artist, to a rigid iconographical scheme. In fact he was free to fill the spaces in the script with whatever he thought fit, and if he wished he could introduce entire pages to illustrate more fully any particular incident. The other artists of the period were more or less compelled to follow traditional designs, and, naturally enough, with the comparative freedom which followed the Iconoclast troubles, they sought their inspiration from the accumulated variety of illustrated books.

The Church of S. Mark at Rossano is an attractive little building, an ivory castle with the merest slits of windows and tiled crenellations. It is simply a cube, surmounted by the drum of a dome at the centre, and by four similar but smaller drummed domes at the corners, all whitewashed, and built on a rock above the town. But as far as this book is concerned, there is nothing remarkable about it that has not already been said of other churches. What is remarkable is that the Normans should not only have countenanced the building of churches for congregations who refused to recognise the Pope and the Western Church, but even contributed to the cost of their erection. For this church, among others, was built in the eleventh century, under the extraordinary tolerance of Norman dominion. There can be no doubt that the Normans must have had a way with them. Not only in England but down here in the south the records are full of their generosity, their broadmindedness, their justice and their faithfulness to existing traditions. Throughout the time of their control, the countries prospered as perhaps never before. The kings acknowledged the religion of the people and ultimately were converted to it : and the people acknowledged the rights of their kings and were converted to their system of government.

PALERMO.

On the way to Palermo the scene of orange trees and lemons, palms and cacti, interspersed with glimpses of the bluest sea, was all so exactly like the Mediterranean of poster and imagination that one hesitated to accept the blatant evidence of one's senses. Crossing from Reggio to Messina, the glimpse of Etna, with a faint wisp of smoke from its cap of snow, seemed to reach the limit of the permissibly picturesque. Yet all along the coast the astonishing palette of colour persists with a kind of exotic irresponsibility, so that

S. MARK, ROSSANO

when one arrived at Palermo one felt already satiated with scenery. Here the hills sweep down to the town and around the bay of sea, encompassing a range of colour unsurpassed by a peacock's tail ; and in the town itself the perennially sunless narrow streets lead to golden squares riotous with semi-tropical vegetation, all tending to give an impression almost too good to be true, but more probably too bewitchingly true to be good.

PALERMO.

Up to now I have purposely avoided mentioning politics and current affairs, except where they were directly concerned with this Byzantine story. For in a travelogue of this nature present events may assume an undeserved prominence, especially when they affect oneself. In March, Mussolini denounced from Rome the English and their fanatical Anglican priests, whose policy it was to propose the imposition of sanctions. The youth of Italy were, he said, fighting for their lives and their country against the cruel Abyssinian aggressor, and yet England suggested imposing sanctions. All this sort of thing does not improve relations between myself and the Italians. No, I am not very popular here. Feelings run high. Mussolini has come to Messina and acclaimed there a part of the might of Italy home on leave. Even at Palermo, over a hundred miles away, it was considered a sufficient occasion for an astonishing flood of posters, post-cards, flags and bunting. Every shop had its portrait, engulfed in swags of green and yellow, every corner its poster and every house its flying colours. At a jeweller's, an unfortunate metal relief of S. Christopher gave way to Il Duce, in the same medium, and in another shop his massive bust nestled in silk hose and green and yellow lingerie, giving him a certain raffish look. Organ grinders played the National Anthem, and soldiers, fascisti and carabinieri trooped the streets in superb uniforms, watched by the topeed warriors on leave in much more tasteful buff.

But to-day the flags are down, S. Christopher has returned to eminence and the posters are covered with black and green caricature portraits of Rubinstein, announcing a piano-forte recital in the near future. The portrait is a crude affair, but seems infinitely preferable to a militant Mussolini.

PALERMO.

The most interesting architecture of Palermo has a peculiar hybrid quality and is quite distinct from the pure Byzantine. The Byzantine simply combined Eastern and Western elements, but the Sicilian Greek added to the already perfected Byzantine something from the Norman West and some more from the Saracen East, to produce a re-markably fine and coherent style. Remarkable, perhaps, because it is so coherent and so clearly defined, and fine because it has taken just those elements of Byzantine, Saracen and Norman which were most suitable for the purpose.

There is a surprising number of churches of the period of Norman kingship, and by far the most picturesque is S. Giovanni degli Eremeti which, with its five red domes, stepped above golden coloured walls, gives an impression of something exotic but un-usually simple, both in line and in form. The domes of the church are unlike anything

Opposite: S. GIOVANNI DEGLI EREMETI, PALERMO

yet described. Unlike the Byzantine, as they do not have the same structural significance ; from the outside they are simply semi-spheres laid on top of the building as a decorative appendage, and as such they are very effective. But they appear to be the result more of a reasoned design than of any constructional necessity. Plastered and painted a pale reddish-brown, the colour of rust, they seem particularly vivid against the persistently blue sky.

The resultant effect does, I believe, justify their addition to the architectural scheme. In this age, when so much of architecture depends on practical needs, the æsthetic need is apt to be overlooked. But surely it is a very real function. As one of the brothers Adam said, in effect, when having one of his designs criticised by a querulous client : " But, madam, you have only to live in it. Think of how many have to pass and see it every day." It is true that the purpose of a building should not be sacrificed in order to achieve an æsthetic effect. They are both important, and the problem is to satisfy both the æsthetic and the practical.

The Church of S. Giovanni is surrounded by charming gardens, and has a cloister of much later date attached to the south side, which adds very well to the general scheme. Inside, the walls only show the bare bones of structural form. If it was ever decorated, there is nothing to show. It has a long nave, divided into bays, each with its dome set on squinches. The window openings, which had seemed small on the outside, are splayed to quite reasonable dimensions inside, to give an entirely adequate light. All are empty but one, that between the first and second bays, which is filled with a delicate grille which looks from a distance like fine embroidery but is discovered, upon examination, to be of pressed stucco and of distinctly Oriental pattern.

PALERMO.

Palermo is surrounded on the south, east and west by an uninterrupted arc of mountains, and set between the mountains and the town is the famous Conca d'Ora, the Golden Shell, which is so wonderfully fertile and stretches for miles with orchards and orange trees laden with fruit to be had for the picking. For the first time I tasted an orange still warm from the heat of the sun and fresh from a tree, which is conveniently enough within a couple of yards of La Piccola Cubola, the object of my visit. Here is the park of Norman kings. Around this royal pleasaunce was constructed a series of artificial lakes, reflecting the palace, the fountains and the kiosks. The Palace of La Cuba has an inscription to distinguish it from the commonplace, and somewhere, I believe, there is a chapel of Byzantine plan. But in the gardens themselves there is La Piccola Cubola, the only example left of the kiosks that were scattered along the edge of the lakes. Four open pointed arches carry a vivid red dome. Architecturally, it might be thought insignificant, but along with the ruins of Tekfour Serai, the palace at Constantinople, it is one of the only examples remaining of Byzantine secular architecture. As such it has an added significance. It is not a ruin, and is simply designed and elegantly proportioned. Altogether it seems pleasant as a garden house, and is very gay in colour ; and no wonder it is gay—the red dome stands sharp against the blue, and the golden arches against the green, in most audacious contrast. All this, within an incomparable setting, tends to give La Piccola Cubola a dramatic as well as an architectural value. But that it *has* an

LA PICCOLA CUBOLA, PALERMO

K

145

architectural value is evident, and as an elementary example of domical design it must be supreme. Nothing could be simpler, and as a garden house nothing could be better.

PALERMO.

" With much love and as a small and unworthy compensation." So runs the inscription in large Greek capitals at the Church of S. Maria dell' Ammiraglio. That was how King Roger's admiral, George of Antioch, dedicated this work. As is usual in a Byzantine plan, it was a square divided into a cross by four columns carrying a dome. But in 1588 came the Renaissance, and the destruction of a great deal of the church. The main front was pulled down and the western arm prolonged to form a Latin cross. A great square took the place of the apsidal end ; and lastly, the work of decoration was entrusted to Guglielmo Borromans. Thanks to this enlargement, the visitor must now endure some thirty feet of Borromans' sticky sentimentality before the Greek cross is reached. Then, having survived all this, what is to be seen ? An odd bit of marble which was once a part of the ikonastasis, a gilt and tinsel altar and some of the finest mosaics in the world. It is possible, too, to get a fair idea of the decorative value of the Byzantine mosaiced church. How very dull and rather futile is the work of Borromans, with his soft, insipid forms and sloppy colouring, alongside the rich, completely determined design of the Byzantine.

I think a part at least of the greatness of Byzantine mosaic lies in the fact that it becomes so much an integral part of the building design, and not merely superimposed decoration. It is this simple unity of structure and design, the luxuriant gamut of colour, the pattern and the texture and the rigid delineation of the subjects which, to me, give the Byzantine mosaics the quality of the truly great. The Byzantine artist was never limited by the more or less outward appearance of things. Like the futurists of more recent art, he endeavoured to portray in one picture not a single incident, but a series, all dependent upon each other. For example, the mosaic in the vault, representing the Nativity, shows several related incidents inside and outside the manger at the same time and in the same composition. The Virgin, and the Child in the crib overlooked by a couple of curious cows, form the principal group, while at one of the lower corners Joseph sits alone on a stool, and at the other two women wash the Infant Christ beside a large basin. Each are separate scenes, parts of the whole. Over all this the shepherds are being informed of the event by the Angels, while the Star of Bethlehem sends a shaft of light, unifying the scene by descending directly to the Christ in the manger.

All Byzantine mosaics possess a dignity and a directness of approach, indeed it is that more than anything which makes this particular art outstanding. Occasionally the drawing is poor, but always it is distinguished from the commonplace by the medium and more particularly by the iconographical limitations imposed on the artist. It is generally recognised to-day that the limitation of medium is good. Things should look what they are. It would be wrong, for instance, to make a wireless set look like a Jacobean commode and in the same way wrong to make mosaic look like painting. Mosaic requires a technique all its own. But limitations as to the arrangement, the colour and even the relative position of a picture in a building is unusual. Nowadays, the artist's development is

S. MARIA DELL' AMMIRAGLIO, PALERMO

ΗΚΟΙΜΗCΙC

S. MARIA DELL' AMMIRAGLIO, PALERMO

S. CATALDO, PALERMO

dependent on the artist, but the latter-day Byzantine accepted a fully developed art backed by centuries of tradition, only occasionally taking a step forward. That he produced great art is only now being recognised, but whether it was due to the artist or to the continued power of tradition and the restrictions of the medium remains in doubt.

PALERMO.

I suppose that in a work of this nature some reiteration is inevitable, and having covered a fair portion of the Byzantine Empire and having grown ecstatic over so much, there comes a time when superlatives must nauseate. Yet invariably they seem to me inadequate. Within this limited vocabulary I search in vain for fresh words that can describe the mosaics of Capella Palatina, the Royal Chapel of King Roger II. And yet they should rank exceedingly high in any inventory of Byzantine artistic achievement. But these words must suffice. Inarticulate, I can at least quote others, contemporary with the building's foundation, who described the mosaics as "gleaming with light, glittering with gold and resplendent with jewels." Gleaming is the right word. These gold mosaics do not need much light and are best lit from above, when they send down gleams of warm, honey colour, illuminating a mosaiced pavement fascinating in its intricacy. But I didn't see it at its best. Like the monastic Church of S. Luke of Stiris, contemporary with this church, the Capella Palatina was partly cluttered with scaffolding. Restoration was in progress in the nave.

However much one may sneer at the present system in Italy, it does at least recognise and look after the invaluable monuments and legacy of the past which are such a source of revenue to the State. While at home we demolish one by one buildings historically and æsthetically great to make way for service flats and super cinemas.

MONREALE.

The tram leaves the Porta Nuova every hour and travels south-west up the steep hill-side. So steep, in fact, that half-way a subsidiary motor is attached to shove us up the remaining stretch. The journey is a tedious one, taking three-quarters of an hour at snail's pace to reach its destination. And the destination is a piazza, faced on three sides with insignificant shops and cafés and on the fourth with the mediocre façade of Monreale Cathedral.

But come inside ; here are mosaics, seventy thousand square feet of them. I may have seen better, but never so much. It is mosaic on such a lavish scale that it overwhelms. Close at hand, they are disappointing, in detail not comparing with the S. Maria della Amiraglio or the Capella.

Of all this area of mosaic, the most outstanding creation is the Christ portrait at the end of the long nave in the conch of the apse. This mosaic dominates the entire iconographical scheme. The one solemn note in a rather gay fantasia. The Head must measure nearly eight feet across ; in the Right Hand is a book inscribed in Latin and Greek, "I am the Light of the World", and the Left Arm sweeps around the apse to bestow a mighty blessing. The Face is that of a severe and omnipotent God, with little of the humble or the lowly. Latin restoration has softened the beard to fluffy brown

S. MARIA DELL' AMMIRAGLIO, PALERMO

wool, but the rest is Byzantine in excelsis, the Power and the Glory, not the Meek and Mild.

On the north wall is a mosaic showing King William receiving his crown from a seated Christ. It follows in all essentials a similar one in the S. Maria della Amiraglio, depicting the coronation of King Roger. The Divine Right of Kings is thus expressed. The true Byzantine monarch generally limited the portrayal of the incident to the imperial coinage. Here the scene is sanctified for all time within the church. And to make doubly sure, William consolidates his position, on the opposite wall, by giving the church to the Virgin.

The Coronation robes of Roger and William are identical; both fantastically bejewelled and distinctly eastern, the costume of an Arabian knight. It may be worth mentioning here that the one is not a copy of the other, nor are they fictitious inventions of the artist, but show the actual Coronation robes. When the tomb of Frederick II (grandson of Roger II) was opened in 1491, and later in 1781, he was found attired in precisely the same bejewelled costume.

It is a pity that William did not follow more closely the Byzantine tradition and have his wife crowned alongside. The Byzantines always did this, the Christ being a taller figure in the centre, holding a crown over each head simultaneously. It would have had a special interest in William's case, for his wife was none other than Joan, sister to Richard Cœur de Lion, King of England.

CASTELVETRANO.

There are two kinds of trains in Sicily, diretto and lento. The diretto stops at every station and the lento wherever the passenger or the engine driver may decide. The time taken by the lento trains is so dependent upon the number of passengers and the sociability of the driver that I must needs travel diretto. But even that is not so quick as one would think. It took three hours to travel from Palermo to Castelvetrano, about sixty miles, only to discover on arrival that my objective was about six kilometres away under the blazing sun.

Walking out of the village and along the country paths, the customary orange and olive groves give place to a vast, rolling patchwork of fields, each ringed with prickly pear, the Sicilian substitute for barbed wire. The little Church of SS. Trinita di Delia bears close resemblance to its contemporaries in Palermo. It is very pleasant, golden coloured, rather solid in appearance, relieved by a series of flat arches and a great red bubble of a dome poised above it. Inside, there is little to see apart from the four columns and their antique caps. Unfortunately, one cannot miss the alien intruder in the form of a pseudo-Renaissance tomb under the dome. A pity, but on the other hand, it is thanks to the Monte Leoni family's munificence that the church has been so carefully restored to house the ancestral bones.

EN VOYAGE.

At Palermo I got the idea of going to Africa. There is something so fantastic in the idea of cutting across to Africa for the day that the opportunity was not to be missed.

153

SS. TRINITA DI DELIA, CASTELVETRANO

Actually it takes just under twelve hours to reach Tunis from Palermo. As things turned out, I was not alone in my idea. Each day one noticed a steady increase of tourist population. Baedekers and Guides Bleus were to be seen at every corner.

So the boat was packed. First class and steerage were thrown into intimate confusion. The fortunate had to clamber over the recumbent to reach their cabins. I must say the stewards did their best, but in the end class distinctions simply had to be abandoned.

A whole hour was spent, and frightful indignities suffered, before we were allowed to leave the boat. We were compelled to queue up for what was called vaccination inspection. Under the impression that it was only necessary to display the scars of previous treatment, jackets were removed and arms bared. But embarrassment increased when it was realised that among the women were some vaccinated in more intimate spots. In a final indignity, the Service Sanitaire Maritime, not satisfied with what we had to show, proceeded with military precision to treat each in turn with scalpel and vaccine.

At last we landed.

TUNIS.

Tunis is noted for remarkably little. The grave of John Howard Payne, one-time Consul for the United States and author of " Home, Sweet Home," and its present prominence along with Corsica and Nice in the Italian Press, alone give it a passing notoriety. But because of its immediate proximity to the ruins of Carthage, it continues to have an importance as a sort of *pied-à-terre* for tourists. The history of the rise of Tunis is coincident with the history of the fall of Carthage. For only one century Carthage was a part of the Byzantine Empire. It was captured by Justinian's general, Belisarius, and given the title Colonia Justinia Carthago. The seat of a bishopric, it was of considerable importance in the early history of Christianity. But during this century of prosperity, Mohamet lived and died, and impelled by his fanatical religious creed, the Arabs captured Carthage in a stride which reached as far as Granada, annihilating at the same time the last stronghold of the North African Church. It was not till the beginning of the nineteenth century that it was discovered that some remote Tuareg tribes still professed the Christian faith. So the Church which had flourished for so short a period in Carthage and was swept away, had prevailed for centuries in the heart of the Sahara Desert. It is indeed remarkable proof, if proof were needed, of the extraordinary tenacity of the Eastern Church whose creed, unaffected by Reformation or schism, has preserved through all the centuries the beliefs of the Byzantine Church as first defined at the Nicene Convention in the presence of Constantine, the first Emperor.

But whatever Tunis may lack in historical associations, it makes up for it and for the tourist by a very plausible Oriental extravaganza. The scene is new and strange and has all the elements and smells commonly associated with the fabulous East. It was only the smells that predominated at Constantinople. But here it all is, sepia complexions and white ducks, like photographic negatives, women in flowing white, masked with black veils, hiding every feature, shuffling along silently. Squatting in the gutter, Arabs with rich, copper faces gaze at arabesques in tattered newspapers. Ragged children scream at us with outstretched hands, begging. Rank and fashion in red fez and immaculate fifty shilling suits sip coffee off brass topped tables outside oriental cafés ; beaten brass, with Sheffield trade marks. Black policemen in solar topees direct the diverse traffic of limousines, umbrella'd cabs, mules and even a camel. This is good—very good indeed. Here is all we had missed at Stamboul ; the costumes, the colour and the sunshine. Orient *à la mode*.

The matt white walls cast deep black shadows across the dusty street. At the end, a horse-shoe arch leads into the Bazaar. Below, the shops are gay with colour and pattern ; above, the façades are studded at intervals with impenetrable latticed grills. And every now and then there are arches flung across the lane, linking either side. Some of these arches are large, vaulted cells, supported by classic columns plundered from ancient Carthage. And along this thoroughfare is ever the silent passing of white-robed, black-veiled women ; in contrast with men, chattering away through the endless sequence of polite formalities and the meaningless courtesies that invariably precede all oriental commerce.

The Bazaar is all in the open, except when under the arched walls. There are men selling red fez hats, piled telescope fashion on the pavement like so many upturned flowerpots ; and vivid striped blankets and deep piled carpets and fabric saddlebags. There are stalls filled with gleaming circles of brass and of copper ; platens, trays and the Sheffield table tops. There are pots and pans, jugs and jars, painted in patterns gaudy and gay. There are leather cushions, fretted and laced in ill-conceived design with brightly coloured thongs. There are astrakhan furs and shaggy sheepskins. There are stalls of fruit, oranges and pomegranates, pyramids of golden spheres. All the colours of the spectrum and more, somehow concentrated within these narrow walls. And ever the silent passing of women, discreetly hooded, and the groups of chattering men.

One more coffee and this interlude is over. Back to the boat, surprisingly enough half empty. And then to the top deck, to see the city and the multitude gathered to watch the ship leave harbour. From whiteness the city dims pink, then soft grey in shade. The waves across the narrow inlet darken. A tiny light flickers for an instant at the pierhead, then grows definite and more vivid as we move towards it. The cold night air drives past and the waves grow bigger as the ship heaves towards the north and the point of Goulette. At last we are in the open sea ; astern, a few lights, then darkness.

CEFALU.

Leaving the hotel at Palermo, another label is stuck on my bag. Another gay rectangle, displaying on this occasion a sunlit palace right on the edge of the Conca d'Ora. The fact that the hotel is situated in a narrow lane for ever sunless and half a mile from the coast does not matter. All that is necessary is a colourful scene, the name of the hotel and the town. Rather like a poster, it has to be striking enough to attract attention. It is a most ingenious system of advertisement, and one in which the immature traveller (myself) gladly plays his part. How ostentatiously one displays these first few tokens of travel. I can think of no other way in which one so willingly plays the part of a commercial traveller. No one would care to carry a case labelled with So-and-So's stomach powder, but one might be quite ready to display the advertisement of the hotel whose cuisine had made the stomach powder necessary. So one might not even have faith in the goods one advertises. But with what blatant snobbery, with what egotistical pride, we show these signs of travel. Perhaps there is something of the souvenir mania in us which makes us retain these mementos of times spent and places seen. But now I learn, from the home of souvenir hunters, that somewhere in 42nd Street assorted labels can be bought, like foreign stamps, unused and in perfect condition, at 50 cents a dozen. So the gilt is off, and one eyes with suspicion every bag that seems to have a surfeit of labels, or more than one's own. Should one give up this collection, clear the case, and encourage no more that eager crowd who twist their necks and read aloud each foreign name? I decide in the train that I should, and later, at a boarding house in Cefalu, the bag is scrubbed for three awful minutes till all is gone except a gilt TA, which is all that is left of Sparta.

Cefalu is famed for its cathedral; not so famed as Monreale, though the cathedral at Cefalu is infinitely better. The measure of fame seems to be in proportion to the measure of distance. If you can afford a taxi you can reach Monreale in under half an hour, but whatever way you go to Cefalu it will take at the very least an hour and a quarter. So a visit to Monreale is more convenient and therefore it is more famous. But that does not mean that Monreale is the better of the two. For it is not. But until travel facilities are simplified, the cathedral at Monreale will bask in an undeservedly lavish amount of fame.

Cefalu is better, I say, the difference being largely that of an original and a copy. For both have the same characteristics of layout and design, and because there is no dome at Cefalu or Monreale neither was obliged to follow any rigid iconographical scheme. And yet they are similar; as like and as different as two chips of the Byzantine block. The same Christ with the open book, the Virgin below and the Apostles below again. Identical arrangements! But drawn at Cefalu with what infinite dignity and power. Here is the work of Greek masters, at Monreale the efforts of the students. There is a tradition to the effect that the mosaics at Cefalu were the work of monks imported by King Roger from Athos, and the quality of the work, along with the introduction of purely Eastern saints, makes this seem a reasonable enough possibility.

NAPLES.

Naples, I am told, is not all that it is cracked up to be. Not by any means. During the long journey to Naples, I had read from a highly coloured pamphlet that " La Bella Napoli is of marvellous beauty, with its gay, careless life surging down its narrow streets, picturesquely enhanced by the occasional vivid glimpses of magic colour of water, earth and sky. Those who see it for the first time are amazed by the exceptional beauty of this enchanted city." And I discovered, too, that if I entered the bay in the evening, I would see " Vesuvius and the sinking sun kissing its fiery summit and the mountain blushing." This last, though not yet verified, I find exceedingly hard to accept. Though it is in no way exceptional to guide book phraseology, mountains do not blush. As for the rest, after a trip around on a one-horse cab, the amazement was not at the enchanted city but at the extravagance of the writer. The custom of guide books to exaggerate is commonplace, but the trouble is that the compilers of travel pamphlets have so indiscriminately scattered every ecstatic adjective that, when one honestly tries to describe something fine or beautiful, there is the danger that the reader will compare it with tourist haunts he has already visited. A sapphire sea ? you say. That's what the book told us of such-and-such a place, and it rained the whole time, turning the sea to lead. The Venice of the North, the Athens of the West, the English Riviera, all are current phrases, the work of authors who, unable to catch the character of the place, must liken it to somewhere else and see everything in the light of rose-tinted spectacles.

The object of this visit was not, however, to praise or decry the city but to see the Cathedral of San Gennaro, and more particularly the Basilica of Santa Restituta, which is attached to the north aisle. Tradition claims that the Basilica was built by Constantine the First in the fourth century from the ruins of the Temple of Apollo ; and there remain in evidence of its antiquity twenty-seven classic columns. Of slightly more recent date are the superb mosaics in a small arched and pointed vault, draped in ragged crimson at one side. Superb they are, with all the grandeur of oriental splendour. The composition is elementary. At the centre, a large and noble Madonna is flanked on either side by the smaller figures of two saints, Gennaro and Restituta. At the base is a carpet on which the Virgin rests her bejewelled feet. No other composition could have been more simple or have filled the arched shape better. The being who sits with such precariousness on the strange perspective of her regal throne is more like an Eastern Empress than the Virgin of Western religion. She sits there with her golden crown, carrying in lieu of a sceptre an elongated and glittering Cross. Robed in a deep and royal blue, lit with lines of gold and shadowed with deep green, she gazes out of her golden vault with cold, mysterious eyes. The small Child she carries vertically in front is only an incidental focus of interest, a small unit emphasising the dignity and glory of His Virgin Mother.

ROME.

The status of Rome in the development of early Christian art is, surprisingly enough, relatively unimportant. For the rise of Christianity was coincident with the political decline of Rome, which resulted in the transfer of the capital of the Empire to Constantinople. Until then, Christianity was not recognised by the State and the Christians were limited to minor craftsmanship upon the walls of the catacombs. This was often the work of the illiterate poor and always devoid of the pomp and circumstance which automatically followed when Christianity became the religion of the Cæsars. Then no longer were the rather dingy underground caverns suitable. Only the temples of the gods were adequate to the new religion ; the greatest in the land must attend Cæsar when he marched in state to divine service. But that was all much later. We are concerned here with the early Christian art of Rome, not with its ultimate development in Constantinople. And this visit has a definite purpose. For it is in Rome, in the strange

158

MOSAICS, NAPLES

catacombs, that much of the earliest of early Christian art is preserved. So far, about fifty catacombs are known, and nearly all are decorated somewhere with mural painting, and some appear to have crypts designed for religious services.

The entrance to the Catacombs of S. Callistus leads down a narrow stair and along a maze of corridors. All is darkness and dripping damp and slimy walls, relieved by the flickering candlelight. We passed innumerable rooms of martyrs' tombs ; walls cut with horizontal niches, one over the other, storey after storey, some fitted with marble slabs bearing indecipherable inscriptions. In all, I am told, five hundred thousand tombs. At last, when the candles we held were getting uncomfortably short, and fingers sheathed in pink wax droppings, we reached a little chapel with a stone altar, and at its side were two frescoed figures, full length, clad in the costume of the period and drawn with ruthless impressionism. After the incomparable delicacy of the Near East, this work has a clumsiness and immaturity that seems at first inexplicable and savage. Cut off from the cultural centre of Rome, the artist displays the crudity of a troubled spirit fighting against great limitations. The figures are heavily outlined in black, and the areas filled with flat colour, giving them a certain decorative value. But though it can never be classed as great painting or even good craftsmanship, it none the less shows quite considerable spiritual expression.

ROME.

Rome, to the student of early Christian art, would have been of first importance had the original Basilica of S. Peter remained. It was built by Constantine over the tomb of the Apostle, and seems to have been an enormous building with five great avenues of columns leading to the altar and to steps which lead down to the sacred " Confessio " of S. Peter below. Across the nave stretched an arch of mosaic, showing S. Peter introducing Constantine to Christ and Constantine in turn presenting Him with a model of the church. Details of this early church survive to tell of its excellence and of the mosaics and the frescoes which covered the walls, inside and outside ; to the front was shown a great Christ, between the Virgin and S. Peter, and below were the Evangelists and the twenty-four Elders, pictured removing their crowns. The work of destruction and reconstruction led to the most interesting discoveries. Bernini was the architect employed to design the present baldachino over the tomb of S. Peter, and his design was for a canopy weighing a hundred tons, supported on four baroque columns, ninety-five feet in height. It will be understood that considerable foundations were necessary to support this weight as well as that of the columns themselves, but it was insisted that the Apostle's remains should not be disturbed. These were in a stone coffin that had been enclosed by Constantine in a great bronze sarcophagus, and on that was laid a golden cross presented by Constantine's mother, Helen. The cross, at least, was seen during the building operations, and there is no reason to doubt that the coffin and cross are still as placed at Constantine's command. In order to avoid tampering with these, each foundation for each column was dug separately ; and within a few inches of the marble paving they started to find coffins and sarcophagii. The ground was thick with the bones and relics of the martyrs.

160

There were found, too, ashes, and bones broken and half burned, which immediately called to mind the great fire of Rome for which Nero, to save his face and acquire power, blamed the Christians, just as Hitler blamed the Communists and the Jews for the conflagration of the Reichstag.

The baldachino, like the rest of S. Peter's, is very much out of scale. By that I mean that the units of the composition do not conform to the customary standards. Buildings may be right, or small, or large in scale. If they are small, they are composed of smaller units than those commonly associated with the human, as in a doll's house. If large in scale, as at S. Peter's, the units are larger and greater ; the balconies, for example, are six feet high and the doors thirty. The result of all this is that the size of S. Peter's cannot be fully appreciated until it is filled with human units. To the visitor, at first, this is a little disconcerting, for he gets the impression that it is much smaller than it really is until he sees that a full grown man does not reach above the first mouldings of the column bases, and seems even then to look like a dwarf.

To me, the only thing worth seeing is Michael Angelo's great dome, a hundred and forty feet in diameter, and, of course, the Pieta. If only Michael Angelo had had the opportunity of carrying out the whole building as he had planned it, how much better it would have been. It was to have taken the form of a Greek cross, but instead it was built by Maderna with a long nave and a massive portico that cuts the dome in half, when seen from the Piazza, and makes it impossible to see the dome complete except from some distance off.

But though the building, when I first saw it, was a disappointment, to-day is Easter Sunday and I at least have had the opportunity of seeing what it looked like filled with people, and of getting some idea of how large it really is. It was fairly early in the morning, at least three hours before the Pope would appear, but already the building was half filled. An hour later the floor was packed tight, except for an avenue down the centre, maintained with difficulty by the Noble Guard, dressed in the uniform of plumed helmets, steel cuirasses, gaily striped doublets and hose, which is supposed to have been designed by Michael Angelo. By the time the Pope's arrival was due, the atmosphere was stifling with the stench of packed humanity, swaying in incessant motion as the density of the crowd increased. The whole pulsating crowd craned their necks westward, pushing or being pushed in the excitement of the moment. Down near the entrance, words of command rang sharply out. And then, to my surprise, followed a piercing fanfare of trumpets from a balcony, heralding the Pontiff's immediate approach. From far off there came cheers and shouts and tumultuous applause. " Papa ! Papa ! " they cried. The moment was at hand. For an instant I saw him far down the nave, a little man in white and gold, perched high on a regal throne, the Sedia Gestatoria, preceded by his personal guard in scarlet jerkins, with drawn swords. And above all this swayed the giant *flabella*, those fans of ostrich feathers which hark back to the time of Constantine and Eastern Imperialism. Slowly the procession crept along the nave. Louder and louder were the " Vivas ! " and the " Papas ! " At last he was not more than twenty feet away ; Pope Pius XI, God's Representative on Earth, a little man with steel-rimmed spectacles, weary with age and illness, bestowed his papal blessing. Behind, in solemn

L

state, walked the cardinals, the bishops and the priests of every order. In this procession was expressed the majesty and the glory of the Church Militant throughout the ages. One was swept aside by the madly cheering crowd. Trumpets and horns blew their loudest. The choir in the east reached crescendo. Priests and nuns, rich and poor, screamed " Papa ! Papa ! " and in this tense excitement let slip their rosaries and breviaries. Somehow, even allowing for the grandeur and the significance of the moment, one couldn't help wondering if they hadn't mislaid their religion too.

CHAPTER EIGHT

IT IS DIFFICULT TO REALISE THAT RAVENNA WAS once a seaport and the headquarters of the Roman Adriatic fleet. For now the sea is six miles away and the crescent harbour which had been reconstructed by the Emperor Augustus is lost beneath centuries of alluvial settlement. Still the sea retires some eight feet each year and, at the same time, surprisingly enough, the ground is sinking six inches per century, so that some of the pavements of the more ancient buildings are below the level of the sea. Unfortunately this means that the present level of the ground is far above the original level, and that the buildings, from the outside, are cut short and appear top heavy. They seem abbreviated and put me in mind of the Scott Monument in Edinburgh, which looks like the great spire of a cathedral which is forever lost beneath the flowers and lawns of Princes Street Gardens. But at Ravenna, all this external inelegance is soon forgotten in the magnificence and the glory of the interiors.

The history of Ravenna, as far as it concerns this study, is divided into three distinct periods of definite character and constitution. The first dates from the beginning of the fifth century and includes the reign of Galla Placidia. The period, in fact, which followed the fall of Rome and the establishment at Ravenna of a new capital of the Western Empire.

Galla, daughter of the Emperor Theodosius the Great, was only twenty when Alaric sacked Rome and took her off as a part of the loot. From that time till she retired to Ravenna, her life was one of extraordinary misfortune. On her alone the mediæval chronicles concentrate, to relieve the dreadful darkness which conceals the last tragic phase of the Western Roman Empire.

When, after a second exile, she finally returned to Ravenna, it was to see her young son crowned at Ravenna and to safeguard his interests. She died about A.D. 450, and was embalmed and placed in her own mausoleum. Up to the sixteenth century she could still be seen through a small hole in the sarcophagus, attired in the imperial purple, seated on a cedar throne. But in 1577, in order to see better, a boy pushed through the hole a lighted taper which set fire to her robes and reduced everything to ashes.

The mausoleum is a little brick building half embedded in the ground. It is cross-shaped in plan, with a dome over the centre which appears outside as a square with a flat pyramidical roof. Inside it is encrusted with mosaics of deepest blue scintillating with gold and silver stars. For such a small building—its length is under thirty feet—it has great richness without being gaudy. Had the walls been covered with gold mosaic it might have looked like a Burma gem shop. But in any case, this building precedes in date the use of great areas of gold.

Over the entrance is Christ, the Good Shepherd, shown here as a beardless youth with long locks of rich brown hair falling on each side. Here is the classic Apollo, the divine youth of early representation. It was not till some time later that the more familiar Christ type came into being. Then, with Christianity elevated to a State religion, it was found necessary for Him to be portrayed as a more awe-inspiring personality, as Lord Triumphant, Controller of the Universe.

There are no authentic portraits of Christ, and it was not till long after His death that any attempt at His portrait was made. And then, of course, it was not based on genuine knowledge of His physiognomy, but on Scriptural interpretation. So it was natural at first that they should assume that the Man who had been followed for three days by a multitude into the wilderness was attractive ; and then, with the knowledge of His everlasting life, to portray Him in the eternal prime of youth. This idea of His appearance was followed throughout the Roman catacombs, sometimes showing Him as a herdsman in the midst of his flock, playing on pipes as Orpheus of old. But here, at Galla's mausoleum, He assumes a more important garb. He is now a regal shepherd, wearing the gold dalmatic as only worn by emperors, and over that a purple gown. It is not till the close of the fifth century that He reaches His supreme status in the Byzantine Empire, when He is seated on a golden throne, wearing an imperial crown and a dark beard, and having as His immediate attendants the saints and the highest dignitaries of the Byzantine Court.

RAVENNA.

For the next seventy-six years after the death of Galla Placidia, the civilisation of Europe was menaced by the great immigrations of the Huns. Already Attila and his savage horde had laid waste some of the Adriatic provinces of the Empire. In the year of her death, Galla had received from Attila an extraordinary message commanding that she should prepare at Ravenna a palace for him, "thy master." Although he conquered a great area, he was eventually turned back, but the years that followed were still shadowed by successive invasions, and in Ravenna only one building survives of the age. This is the Baptistry, which had been adapted from a thermal chamber that had once been a part of the Roman Baths. Up till then, it was customary to perform the apostolic rite of baptism at river sides, in the open. But the Roman Baths, with their admirable plumbing, would obviously be more acceptable to the neophyte. And so from the banks of the river the ceremony was transferred to the seclusion and comparative comfort of the thermæ.

The second great period opens with the capture of Ravenna by Theodoric the Austrogoth in 493. This was followed by thirty years' peace and great building activity.

ARIAN BAPTISTRY, RAVENNA

Theodoric informs his architect that he wishes to illustrate his age with many new edifices which should be the admiration of new generations of men, and that it is the duty of the architect to fulfil his lively desire. Of the buildings that still remain is a second Baptistry on much the same lines as the earlier one. This, too, is covered with mosaics, and on the dome appear the Apostles and Prophets, radiating from a central composition of a stark Christ, still beardless, being baptised by a very rugged S. John. And, as if to show that even the Roman gods had recognised the Christian faith, we find Neptune reclining against an upturned jar beaming his approval over the entire proceedings.

Theodoric had another ambition in addition to evoking by his buildings the admiration of future generations, and that was to resemble the great Roman Emperors. But because of his Arian beliefs he was regarded contemptuously by the Church of Rome. These beliefs, which suggested that Christ the Son, though Divine, was quite a different person from His Father, had already been condemned at the Council of Nicea in A.D. 325. In any case, the Romans were pleased to remind Theodoric, with his imperialistic ideas, that there was already an emperor, Augustus Justin, at Rome. In the later years of his life, many unfortunate persecutions estranged him finally from the Orthodox Church at Constantinople, so that all his greatness and his triumphs were suppressed.

Theodoric, in imitation of the earlier Roman emperors whom he so much admired, built for himself a mausoleum, and this mausoleum is a remarkable monument. Externally it has all the attraction that Galla's mausoleum lacks. The main structure is round, elevated on a dodecagonal basement. The interior, which is bare, is lit by small holes high up in the drum. Above is the most remarkable feature of all. A great dome, carved from a solid block of Istrian marble, a hundred and seven feet in circumference, three feet thick and, I am informed, four hundred and seventy tons in weight. Radiating from the centre on the outside are carved massive handles, inscribed with the names of the Apostles, from which it is assumed the stone was lowered on to the drum. So we have a quite new construction. The dome is simply a dead weight, exerting no outward thrust, resting on the drum like the lid on a dustbin. Simple enough, but always limiting the size of the building to the size of the covering stone.

RAVENNA.

Diplomatic relations, which had been difficult during the closing years of Theodoric's reign, were finally broken off, after a series of unfortunate incidents, by the Emperor Justinian in 534. The Vandals had by this time control of the African coast, and it was there that Justinian's great armies struck first. Under the great General Belisarius they entered Carthage. From there Justinian's army struck north to Sicily, Naples, Rome, and finally, after some underhand negotiation, they entered Ravenna. From now on, for over two hundred years, it remained in the Byzantine Empire, the seat of an Exarch, subject only to Constantinople. Towards the end of the eighth century it was lost to the newly crowned Charlemagne, rival emperor in the west, who seems to have used it as a sort of art store to be plundered at will, to inspire barbarian art at Aix-la-Chapelle.

The reason for this outburst of historical data is to explain the extraordinary mosaics of the Church of S. Apollinare Nuovo. The title is misleading, for the church was

built by Theodoric round about 526, and the reason the mosaics seem extraordinary is that they show in the same building, on the same walls, work of two distinct and completely discordant periods. The two upper rows of simple early Christian pictures are of Theodoric's time, while below, dominating the whole, is expressed in a great imperial pageant of martyrs, virgins and saints the might and the glory of the religion of the Byzantine State. They link, in fact, the period of Theodoric with the period of Justinian.

Somehow one cannot help feeling that the later mosaics were really placed there to emphasise the might of the new empire builders. For reasons of state, as it were ; not to beautify Theodoric's church, which was already complete, but to contrast the insignificance of his little pictures with the magnificent religious display of the Byzantine Empire that was now here to guard the city's interests. These mosaics are unlike anything yet seen. They express the atmosphere of a court reception rather than the eternal mystery of the Church ; but the subjects are religious even if they appear at first sight faintly secular. The Virgin is enthroned on the north wall, Christ on the south. Both are attended by Angels, and conclude the procession to the altar of threescore virgins and saints. The sequence of figures, all clad in white, is relieved by the introduction of date palms, rising between each one, which gives the composition a simple rhythmic quality. It is the feeling of rhythm, which emphasises the length of the nave of the basilica, that makes the mosaics so important to the architectural scheme. Later, with the restrictions of the iconographical code, such continuity was impossible, but by this time the Byzantines had evolved a new domed architecture and processional mosaics were no longer necessary. The aim eventually was the unity of the whole ; art and architecture were merged to produce a great and enduring expression of a constant religious impulse.

The mosaics of S. Apollinare Nuovo are of great interest to the student of Christian art not only because of the beauty of their execution but because they represent the earliest list of martyrs in the history of Christian art. On the left, the women's side of the church, are the female martyrs, all clad alike, marching towards the Virgin in single file, distinguished from each other by the names written above them ; on the right, the males, similarly identified, lead towards the Christ, who is seen here for the first time bearded and enthroned in the Byzantine manner. The haloes of the martyrs are simple coloured lines, those of the Virgin and her attendant angels solid gold discs.

The origin of this peculiar device which distinguishes the saintly from the ordinary mortal is hard to find. The halo is commonplace in Hindu art, it was often used in early pagan iconography, and was frequently given to Roman Emperors. It has been suggested that it owes its origin to the metal plates that were sometimes placed over the heads of classic statues to protect them from the weather and incontinent birds. But by the sixth century its use had become universal in Christian art, and relative degrees of importance were characterised by different types of haloes. Living mortals were generally represented by square haloes, only the emperors, retaining their traditional divinity, by a saintly circlet.

RAVENNA.

The historian and the archæologist would, I suppose, prefer Constantinople as a centre for Byzantine research. But, their interests are antiquarian, and their enthusiasm depends,

CHAIR OF MAXIMIANUS, RAVENNA   169

S. APOLLINARE IN CLASSE

S. VITALE, RAVENNA

more or less, on how old a thing is, not on how beautiful an old thing is. (Of course old things are not necessarily beautiful, but my concern has been with those which I believe to be both old and beautiful.) Ravenna, then, to the student of Byzantine art, offers the finest examples of the craftsmanship of Constantinople. There is, for instance, the magnificent chair of the Archbishop Maximianus, which displays on its side the finest of all ivory carvings. Then there are the mosaics at the basilica of S. Apollinare in Classe and in the Archbishop's Chapel, all deserving more than a mention. Even the chair alone would have made Ravenna worth visiting ; but all fade to mediocrity before Justinian's great church. We have seen at S. Sophia great architecture unadorned, the very essence of simplicity in design and coherent form. Here, at S. Vitale, is passable architecture, but enriched with the unrestrained luxury of mosaic on an imperial scale.

Within this wealth of mosaic the eye is carried, not as usual to the dome, but to the apsidal end. Here is Christ, seated on a pale blue globe and flanked by massive black-haired angels. Further down the apse are two compositions, the finest mosaics of the finest period of the Empire. On the right is Justinian, the most noble of all the Cæsars, carrying, for some reason, a golden dish, and alongside him are Maximianus, some priests and a posse of soldiers. Attired in purple and gold, crowned with the imperial diadem and outstanding in the group because of his saintly halo, he leers across the apse to the second composition and his wife Theodora. Theodora, whose profession, in an age of discretion, has been euphemistically described as that of an actress, stares back wide-eyed ; surrounded by the ministers of the Court, she stands, a beautiful, painted goddess, sparkling with jewels and, like her husband, is alone distinguished by a spangled halo. So the imperial pair take their places in eternity with all the Saints, the Archangels and the almighty hierarchy. The faces, which are drawn with meticulous detail, are apparently true portraits, and both compositions seem to have been studied with such care that they have great importance to the student of costume, giving one a fair idea of the fashions of the Imperial Court in the most important epoch of the Byzantine Empire.

THE PIAZZETTA DEI LEONI, VENICE.

My room is high above a small square and the constant murmur of people passing by. The window leads to a terrace, and there I can see across the little piazza to the domes of S. Marco. Each morning I sit there and have my coffee and share my brioche with the pigeons. At all times of day they are fluttering about the terrace until nightfall, when they add to the undertone of the crowds and the distant clatter of cups and plates from Florian's with a soft and low purling monotone.

At S. Marco the big candles by the altar have been extinguished, and only a few people remain at the side chapels and the confessionals ; all the crowds of tourists have gone back to their hotels and their tables d'hote and there is peace at last in the misty twilight. The great dome, lit in the last light of the sun, is reflected on the floor like a golden pool in the centre of a strange and shadowless grey.

I have been here the better part of the day and have seen these vast areas of colour and light on the walls change with the passage of the sun till they sank finally into this deep and impenetrable obscurity. I have seen these mosaics close at hand from the

JUSTINIAN, RAVENNA

galleries and I have watched over the floor when it seemed alive with the movement of people. I have seen the great bronze horses which had once stood over Nero's triumphal arch and later at the vast Hippodrome in Constantinople. I have seen in the Treasury the plunder of the Crusades, the gold and silver model of Sancta Sophia, the agate and alabaster chalices and the jewelled relics of the East.

I saw all these, and now that I have returned to my room I cannot help wondering what words would express adequately so much. I cannot praise. But I can curse. I can curse the Renaissance and the growth of Latin materialism which has disfigured so much of S. Marco. The sincere religious beliefs which created S. Marco are overwhelmed by the proximity on these walls of frightful horrors applied in the age of Venetian commercialism.

I have already said that Byzantine decoration was introduced on the walls of the churches mainly for instructional reasons. This gave the mosaics and the frescoes a purely functional value. Then I have tried by illustration and description to indicate how, with an educational aim, the Byzantines created a coherent and easily understood style in art. In producing these instructional pictures they always recognised the limitations of whatever medium they used. When they worked in mosaic they thought in terms of compositions made from innumerable glass cubes and designed accordingly. And that is as it should be. Good art is always subject to the medium of its execution. A good painting, whatever its significance to the beholder, should look like a painting ; and good mosaic, quite apart from its educational importance in the eyes of the Byzantine, should look like mosaic. But at S. Marco one sees mosaics, products of the Italian Renaissance, which are horrible and grotesque ; simply bad painting transmuted to glass mosaic. Here, over these Byzantine vaults, are massive sexless cherubs in white and gold, supported on verdant pastures, like so many fried eggs on spinach. Great flabby flutters of vague and ill-conceived upholstery cover the vast arches and ooze outside to the portico walls in a nightmare of infinite disorder. It is all so ostentatious and so insincere. In that age when art became a commercial product, the Byzantines lost their place in this world, Constantinople fell and their art in the West, to all intents and purposes, died.

Of the original Byzantine front, only one mosaic remains. The rest follow the pompous fashion of concentrated superficialities and saccharine sweetness. But the one which has been preserved, by a kind of fate, shows us the church as it was in 1204, then completed ; it shows the arrival of S. Mark at his final resting place ; his haloed head peeping over the edge of the coffin to see the great cortege of kings and queens, priests and officiating clergy who form his escort. And above tower the arches and domes of the church, the church of Byzantine times, independent of its sugar pinnacles and marble bijouterie. The church as it then was. The church which, we are informed, had followed so closely the lines of Justinian's Church of the Holy Apostles at Constantinople ; and the church which, in its turn, had been copied by the French in Aquitaine. It is a link between the extraordinary domed churches of southern France and the Greek achievement three thousand miles east. It explains how, at a time when the Normans were still involved in elementary barrel vault construction, there appeared in France that completely alien and fully developed style.

S·MARCVS

NIFICES·CLERVS·PPLS·DVXᴹTE·SERENVS·LAVDIB;AǪ·CHORIS·EXCIᴾ

MOSAICS, S. MARK, VENICE

S. MARK, VENICE (EXTERIOR)

S. MARK, VENICE, PORTICO

177

M

TORCELLO.

It was the habit of the more friendly writers on Venice to maintain in their literary efforts an air of great affection for the reader. " Come with me," one would write, " and sit in my gondola, for we are going to Torcello to see the lovely things there." But to-day it is all very different. If you want to come with me to Torcello you'll take the paddle steamer and be lucky if you get a seat at all. Even so it will be worth while if only to get away for a time from all the dull and superficial trivialities that have spoiled so much of S. Marco at Venice. You will see at Torcello as lovely a mosaic as any produced by the Greeks on their native soil ; a solitary, blue-robed Virgin standing full height on a vast field of gold mosaic, gazing above you like some distant goddess imbued with a mysterious and eternal dignity. And you will see on the low chancel screen a sculptured panel of two peacocks face to face which, if not anatomically sound, do at least combine to produce as exquisite a piece of carving as one could find throughout the Empire. And if all that is not good enough, dear reader, then climb the campanile and you will get a view over this bare little island, over the lagoons and over to Venice, the view that Ruskin thought " one of the most notable in this wide world of ours ".

CHARTRES.

The almost complete absence of sculpture in stone and marble in the history of Byzantine art has already been remarked. The eastern sculptor's abhorrence of any representation of the human figure in the round was the natural result of this new religion which forbade the construction of idols. Instead, as we have seen, they drew flat, elongated symbols of people that were full of dignity but could never be called human. They glorified the ascetic as their forefathers had idealised the athletic.

But in the more intimate and minor arts, as in the carving of steatite and ivory, the same revulsion to human representation is not so evident. On the contrary, great quantities of ivory carvings showing figures in the round or in high relief were produced throughout the period of the Empire, so that these ivories link the sculpture of ancient Greece with the mediæval achievements in the West. Alone, through centuries of barbarism in Europe, Constantinople had preserved and promoted her artistic inheritance from Greece and Rome and coupled a vast culture from further east. When the time of comparative peace came, relations between Constantinople and the West seemed to have been very friendly. Works of art, as gifts to the courts of Europe, were the customary diplomatic merchandise. Long before the Crusaders returned with the booty of Constantinople, many ivories and manuscripts had been exported to the West. These works of art had already exerted a considerable influence over the artistic development of England, France and Germany. At Chartres we find the production of a fully developed art as early as 1150. The sculptures of the western portals, to me the supreme expression of the stone-carver's art, give evidence of the extent of Byzantine influence. From nowhere else at that time could the inspiration have been derived. The same elongation of figure evident in fresco and manuscript, the same fine graven lines and rigid limitation of shape obvious in an ivory carving, seem to have been somehow adapted here in stone, and done with a superb skill and craftsmanship never emulated by the

178

MARBLE CARVING, TORCELLO

Byzantine. But then the Byzantines consecrated their art to their religion and their religion would not permit graven images. So the sculptors in stone and marble were limited to low reliefs, an occasional secular bust and the design of column capitals, which at least they did very well. But Chartres is sculpture on a monumental scale. There are in the western portals alone, I am told, some seven hundred and twenty figures, large and small, and each is an exquisite unit in itself. Such magnificence cannot be paralleled in the Near East, nor, I believe, in the West.

LE RETOUR.

As I look back over these patchwork notes, I cannot help wondering if they follow any discernible pattern. Do the silken patches, for instance, shine out in true proportion to the rest ? Or does their importance seem lost alongside the gaudy cretonnes which suffer from a surfeit of superlatives ? It would not surprise me if they did ; for in a diary of this sort all order and arrangement is subject to geographical rather than historical sequence. The story follows the simplest and most economically arranged tour that could be managed. I determined, as far as possible, not to tell of things I had read of but had not seen. Everything was new to me and apart from a few book illustrations I knew nothing of what lay ahead. It was during the tour that each patch was added to this Byzantine pattern, so that it is only now that I can look back over it all and, seeing the result as a whole, trace the essential unity.

Here and there the patches are linked with thin threads of historical data. Threads which are, of course, important, but only so far as they help to keep the patches together. For I have concentrated more on the æsthetic appeal of Byzantine art than on the historical story. The history of the Empire, like all histories, makes sad reading. It is little more than a record of crime, folly and misfortune. It does not tell of the greatness of the Byzantines and gives very little clue to their art or their religion. Only a tour of this nature, it seems to me, can give one a real insight into the art of any country, of any epoch. This patchwork is only a record of how that tour impressed itself on my mind. To any reader it can give no more than an impression of something that impressed profoundly someone else.

RUTHWELL.

The gap between the journey's end and this summer day has been occupied in correcting in the script errors of fact and errors of grammar, an occupation which involved the study of a great many books ; books which were so often couched in such erudite phraseology as to be unreadable ; books which had remained for so long on topmost library shelves that one could almost calculate by the thickness of the dust that lay upon them the number of decades that had lapsed since they were last disturbed ; books obtained through the Central Library for Students, partly burned and with sodden leaves that told of the Blitz and the great fire over London. But when they were read and this work was done, there remained one place which, in a world at war, was still accessible and would at least round off this journey. And this place lay near at hand, within, in fact, two hours' journey of the factory in which I was employed.

Ruthwell, on the Solway Firth, is a good enough place to conclude this work. It possesses the finest stone cross in the world. Even the Baron Baedeker, who is so sparing

of asterisks in his Scottish Guide, is enthusiastic. It is here we find the most important link between the Early Christian Greek and this homeland; a carved sandstone cross, seventeen and a half feet high, tapering slightly from a base nearly two feet square, carved on the sides with the grape-vine scroll and on the front and back with figure compositions which are derived exclusively from the Christian East. These pictures in stone are explained by Latin inscriptions, and Runic letters are introduced down the sides as a border to the vine. These Runic letters, which are a debased Greek designed to suit carving, present certain difficulties in translation. They were first interpreted by a Mr. Repp, who announced that they told of a baptismal font presented to the Therfusian Fathers in compensation for their loss of thirteen cows and the damage done to the fields in the Vale of Ashlafar. This was a correct reading of the letters assuming that the Runes were translated into Scandinavian, and as the inscription is not split into words, Repp was free to make his own combinations. A Mr. Kemble eventually found a more likely, and apparently correct, solution. He discovered in the library at Piedmont an old Anglo-Saxon skin book, inscribed with the lines of an ancient poem which, when translated into Runic, tallied with the characters on the Cross. It was a poem, " The Dream of the Holy Rood ", written by Cædmon in the seventh century, and at the top of the Cross, much worn away, are the Runes which, construed, read " Cædmon Made Me ".

RUTHWELL.

I have tried, as far as possible in this book, to avoid undue mention of current affairs. This has been purely a travelogue, an attempt to study at first hand some of those places where Byzantine art had still endured. But for the moment, with the sole exception of Constantinople, the entire area I have covered is in German hands. I cannot help thinking back to Athos, which had for so long prevailed under the heel of Moslem domination. Surely the Mountain will survive this more temporary phase. I wondered what happened to the monks at Meteora, who maintained their culture so high above the land on such singular limestone pinnacles. What has become of all these communities, who devoted their lives to the preservation and continuance of early Christian beliefs and customs which were once the primary source of European culture and intellectual thought? "The bulwark of civilisation! The guardians of Christendom!"

And what of Mistra? That romantic ruined city—is it still in the care of those six gallant ladies? For upon their efforts the preservation of some of the most exquisite paintings in the world depends. Do they still, I wonder, go out at dusk with their little lamps which they place so carefully in the centre of the church, trying to keep the frescoes dry? Maybe that is all past now. Maybe they don't even get the oil to fill their tiny lamps. Maybe these six nuns, who were such happy ladies, are not able to look after them any more. Maybe, in that dreadful struggle for Greece, it has all been blasted to hell by German artillery. But it is better not to dwell too long on these unhappy, uncertain thoughts.*

Now the sky darkens over the Solway, leaving only a slash of light across the west and the north. The tidal waters rise steadily, so that the great stretches of mud and sand, which we had walked across in the heat of the day, are now broken into innumerable islands by a vast system of ever increasing rivers.

It is cold and singularly quiet. We sit on the bank and watch the tide rise and see the moon rise with it. Then, far across the indeterminate grey, some cattle, stranded in midstream, low pathetically and retreat to the temporary security of one of the new formed islands. And as the even perimeter decreases they crowd together, closer, closer, till the island is lost beneath them as though from the sheer concentrated weight of cows. From the farm come collie dogs and a herdsman, but the dogs are afraid and the herdsman can only shout. At last one cow steps forward, is caught up by the stream and starts to swim her way across the driving current. The others follow suit and the whole lot are eventually being swept towards the sea, but always getting a little nearer the safe coastline. They reach safety, about a couple of hundred yards further down, and the dogs are no longer afraid and snap at their legs, and the herdsman gives a hoarse laugh and drives the cattle off towards the dark lands and the shadowy beaches.

* The nuns are still there, and Mistra is as lovely as it ever was.

APPENDIX

The notes which follow have been made in order to show the relationship between the ground covered by this journey and the framework of the Byzantine Empire as a whole. They aim at giving the general reader a brief guide to the outstanding characteristics of Byzantine architecture, indicating how it came into being, how it developed, and how its influence persisted long after the Empire itself had passed away.

THE HISTORICAL BACKGROUND

The chart on the following two pages indicates the general developments of the Empire in relation to events in Eastern and Western Europe. Items of especial significance in the development of the Byzantine Empire are indicated in heavier type.

CAUSE

DATE	IMPORTANT PERSONS, ETC.	IMPORTANT EVENTS
0	Augustus Cæsar (29 B.C.–A.D. 14)	**Birth of Christ** Crucifixion, A.D. 30 Missionary activities of S. Paul, A.D. 37–66
	Nero (A.D. 54–68)	Fire of Rome—Persecutions of Christians, A.D. 64
100	Trajan (A.D. 98–117)	Roman Empire at greatest extent, A.D. 117
	Hadrian (A.D. 117–138)	
200		
	Caracalla (A.D. 211–217)	
300	Diocletian (A.D. 284–305) *Dynasty of Constantine* (A.D. 303–378) **Constantine the Great** (A.D. 303–337)	Persecutions of Christians, A.D. 303 Edict of Milan, A.D. 313 Council of Nicea, A.D. 323
	St. Augustine (A.D. 354–430) **Julian the Apostate** (A.D. 361–363) *Theodosian Dynasty* (A.D. 379–457) **Theodosius the Great** (A.D. 379–395)	**Foundation of Constantinople,** A.D. 330
400		Goths under Aleric capture Rome, A.D. 410 **Great wall of Constantinople,** A.D. 413
	Leonine Dynasty (A.D. 457–518) **Leo I** (A.D. 457–474)	Gothic invasions of Italy, Spain and N. Africa, A.D. 420–440 Foundation of Venice, A.D. 432
500	**Belisarius** (A.D. 505–565) *Justinian Dynasty* (A.D. 518–601) **Justinian the Great** (A.D. 527–565)	
	Mohammed (A.D. 569–632)	**Italy, Spain and N. Africa captured by Belisarius,** A.D. 530–540 **Ravenna seat of Exarch,** A.D. 539 **Byzantine Empire at greatest extent,** A.D. 560 Lombards conquer N. Italy except Ravenna and Rome, A.D. 565
600		
	Heraclean Dynasty (A.D. 610–717)	**Moslems capture Syria and Jerusalem,** A.D. 634
700		**Moslems capture Egypt and destroy Carthage,** A.D. 692–698
	Isaurian Dynasty (A.D. 717–867) **Leo III (Iconoclast)** (A.D. 717–802)	**Moslems invade Spain,** A.D. 710 **Leo orders removal of all sacred images,** A.D. 725 Moslems defeated at Poitiers in France, A.D. 732
	Charlemagne (A.D. 742–814)	
800	*Armorian Dynasty* (A.D. 820–867)	Charlemagne crowned by Pope at Rome, A.D. 800 **Moslems capture Sicily and S. Italy,** A.D. 831
	Macedonian Dynasty (A.D. 867–1057)	**End of Iconoclastic controversy,** A.D. 843
900		
1000	Vladimir of Russia (A.D. 956–1015)	**Recognition of Greek Church by Russia,** A.D. 989
	Ducas Dynasty (A.D. 1059–1081)	**The Great Schism between Greek and Latin churches,** A.D. 1054 Normans capture England, A.D. 1066
	Comnenian Dynasty (A.D. 1081–1185)	**Normans capture Sicily and S. Italy,** A.D. 1070 Revival of Islam under the Seljuk Turks, A.D. 1071
1100		First Crusade, A.D. 1095
		Second Crusade, A.D. 1147
	Innocent III, Pope (A.D. 1160–1216) Francis of Assisi (A.D. 1182–1226) *Angelus Dynasty* (A.D. 1185–1204) Saladin, Sultan of Egypt (A.D. 1187–1193) *Lascarid Dynasty* (A.D. 1204–1261) Kublai Khan (A.D. 1216–1294) Thomas Aquinas (A.D. 1225–1274) *Paleologue Dynasty* (A.D. 1258–1453) Dante Alighiere (A.D. 1265–1337) Giotto (A.D. 1266–1337)	Saladin captures Jerusalem, A.D. 1187 Third Crusade, A.D. 1189 **Fourth Crusade—Capture of Constantinople,** A.D. 1204 Fifth Crusade, A.D. 1217 Sixth Crusade, A.D. 1228 Seventh Crusade, A.D. 1248 **Greeks regain Constantinople,** A.D. 1261
1200		
1300	Chaucer (A.D. 1340–1400)	Norman dominion in Sicily ends, A.D. 1296 **Ottoman Turks cross to S.E. Europe,** A.D. 1306
1400		**Ottoman Turks capture Sophia,** A.D. 1385 **Ottoman Turks capture Salonika,** A.D. 1430 **Ottoman Turks capture Constantinople,** A.D. 1453
	Constantine XI (A.D. 1448–1453)	**Ottoman Turks capture last outposts of Empire,** A.D. 1461 Columbus discovers America, A.D. 1492
1500	Ivan (The Terrible) (A.D. 1547–1584) Richelieu (A.D. 1585–1642)	Holy League against Turks, A.D. 1571

EFFECT

POLITICAL, RELIGIOUS, AND SOCIAL DEVELOPMENTS

Period of Imperial Roman expansion. Christianity, carried by S. Paul to Rome, is regarded as a seditious religion because its adherents, like the Jews, would not recognise the divinity of Cæsar. Nevertheless it takes root throughout the Roman Empire, particularly in the East. The persecution of Christians is inaugurated by Nero, who accuses them of firing Rome.

Rome's extensive frontiers are constantly menaced. Central government control of furthest outposts is difficult, and leads to quasi-partition. Italian agriculture declines and Italy becomes an impoverished land of slaves, maintaining a great underpaid army of mercenaries. Rome is no longer the social or economic heart of the Empire and the need is felt for a new administrative centre further from the western barbarians and nearer the wealthy eastern colonies. Diocletian takes the first step, establishing political centres at Nicomedia and Spalato. Persecutions under his reign fail to suppress Christianity. Ten years after Constantine's accession, Christianity is recognised by the Edict of Milan, and following on his conversion Christianity is established as State religion. All competing faiths are swept away or absorbed. The simple ceremonials of the early Church are replaced by pomp and magnificence. Pagan temples are frankly converted into Christian churches. **Constantine completes the work begun by Diocletian by founding a new capital at Byzantium in the East which is the Christian capital of the Roman Empire.**

After the transfer of the capital to Byzantium (Constantinople), the Empire is subject to more and more eastern influences. Consolidation of eastern power involves war with Persia, and at the same time Italy and Constantinople are being subjected to invasion from the North. Italy is lost, and Rome is sacked by Aleric, but Constantinople is saved by Theodosius, who strengthens the city walls. Italy and North Africa having fallen to the barbarians, Constantinople alone preserves the culture of Europe.

During a period of comparative peace in the West, rivalry springs up between the Greek and Latin Churches. Doctrinal disputes and the claim of the Pope to the headship of the entire Christian Church cause a rift which is the beginning of a series of dissensions.

Under Justinian, the western half of the Empire is temporarily regained by General Belisarius. The Empire is now at its greatest extent, and includes all North Africa and Spain. It is a period of great building activity, particularly in Constantinople and Ravenna. Byzantine architecture has now developed clearly distinguishing characteristics. The period of control is soon lost to the Lombards.

Mohammed's successor plans to subjugate the world and convert it to Islam. **The Byzantine army is shattered in** A.D. **634 and the Empire loses Syria, Palestine and Egypt.**

The Moslems carry their conquest to W. Europe and are eventually defeated in France. In the West, under the influence of Latin Christianity and early feudalism, there is a period of political and social consolidation, culminating in the coronation of Charlemagne as rival Emperor. **In Constantinople, under Leo III, no representation of the divine or saintly form is permitted. This leads to bitter controversy and results in many artists being compelled to leave the Empire and find employment in the West, where they exert considerable influence on Carolingian art.**

During the ninth century Sicily and S. Italy are lost to the Saracens, but within the Empire the latter part of the century and the beginning of the next is a period of recuperation. Syria and Mesopotamia are regained from the Moslems, and in 988 the Orthodox religion spreads to the newly constituted Russian states. This prefaces a period of remarkable architectural activity, centred first at Kief, later at Novgorod and lastly Moscow under Ivan the Terrible. The influence of Byzantine Constantinople persists in Russia long after the capital falls.

During the eleventh century a permanent break is made between Greek and Latin Churches when the two Pontiffs excommunicate each other. It is a period of religious enthusiasm in the West which leads to a series of Crusades aimed at gaining, for the Church, power in the East. The century is notable for the rise of two great powers : (1) in the West the Normans, who, after capturing England, follow with the invasion of Sicily and S. Italy, where they develop the legacy of Byzantine and Saracen culture ; **and (2) in the East the Seljuk Turks, who invade Asia Minor, defeating the Byzantine army in 1071.**

The Crusades open up new trade routes between East and West. The power of Venice grows with expanding trade. Venice rivals Constantinople. **The fourth Crusade, financed by Venice, is directed against Constantinople, which is sacked and looted** (A.D. 1204). **A Latin Prince rules at Constantinople, but the Imperial line is maintained at Nicæa.** The plunder of Constantinople stimulates craftsmanship and the Renaissance of Learning in Italy and Western Europe.

Constantinople is regained (A.D. 1261), **but the Empire is considerably diminished owing to the loss of Dalmatia and the encroachment of new Moslem tribes in the East.**

The days of the great Emperors have passed. The Empire is now impoverished and fighting a losing battle against the advancing Turks, who in 1306 cross to Europe ; in 1422 they lay siege to Constantinople, and thirty-one years later capture the city. The Turks sweep on, taking Athens (1456), Trebizond (1461), Mistra (1462), and are finally repulsed at Vienna in 1683.

Ivan the Terrible, claiming kinship with the Paleologue family, declares Moscow as Third Rome and assumes the title of Cæsar (Czar).

Refugees from Constantinople flee westward, where civilisation now flourishes. In France a descendant of the last Constantine, supported by Cardinal Richelieu, develops the idea of a further Crusade to regain the Empire from the Turks, but the scheme is frustrated with the beginning of the Thirty Years' War in Europe (A.D. 1619).

IMPORTANT BUILDINGS

Temple of Castor and Pollux, Rome (A.D. 6)

The Colosseum, Rome (A.D. 70–82)

The Pantheon, Rome (A.D. 120)

Thermæ of Caracalla, Rome (A.D. 212–235)

Palace of Diocletian, Spalato (A.D. 300)
Arch of Constantine, Rome (A.D. 312)
Church of the Nativity, Bethlehem (A.D. 3)

Basilican Church of S. Peter's, Rome (A.D. 330)

S. George, Salonika (A.D. 400)
Mausoleum of Galla Placidia, Ravenna (A.D. 420)
S. Maria Maggiore, Rome (A.D. 432)
S. John of the Studion, Constantinople (A.D. 463)
S. Apollinare Nuovo, Ravenna (A.D. 493–525)
S. Demetrius, Salonika (A.D. 500–550)
San Vitale, Ravenna (A.D. 526–547)
SS. Sergius and Bacchus, Constantinople (A.D. 527)
Tomb of Theoderic, Ravenna (A.D. 530)
Sancta Sophia, Constantinople (A.D. 532–537)
S. Apollinare in Classe, near Ravenna (A.D. 534–539)
S. Sophia, Salonika (A.D. 560)

S. Irene, Constantinople (A.D. 740)

Aix-la-Chapelle Cathedral (A.D. 796–804)

Kapnikarea, Athens (A.D. 875)

S. Mark's, Venice (A.D. 1042–71)
S. Theodore, Athens (A.D. 1049)
S. Saviour in the Chora, Constantinople (A.D. 1050)
S. Theodore, Constantinople (A.D. 1100)
S. Fosca, Torcello (A.D. 1108)
S. Front, Perigueux (A.D. 1120)
Capella Palatina, Palermo (A.D. 1132)
S. Sophia, Trebizond (A.D. 1143)
Monreale Cathedral (A.D. 1147)
S. Cataldo, Palermo (A.D. 1161)

Salisbury Cathedral (A.D. 1220–58)
Metropole, Athens (A.D. 1250)

Pantanassa, Mistra (A.D. 1400)
Pazzi Chapel, Florence (A.D. 1429)

S. Peter's, Rome (A.D. 1506–1626)
Dochiariou, Mount Athos (A.D. 1550)
S. Basil, Moscow (A.D. 1555–60)

TYPICAL GREEK CHURCH TO THE SAME SCALE

NORTH EAST SIDE OF SANCTA SOPHIA

SOME NOTES
ON THE CHURCH OF SANCTA SOPHIA

Sancta Sophia (*Αγιος Σοφια* = Divine Wisdom) was built by Justinian and dedicated in 537. It stands on the site of two earlier basilican churches of the same name, which in their turn were probably erected on the site of an early Greek temple to Pallas Athene. It was partly destroyed by earthquake in 558, and restored in 563. Minor additions and restorations took place in the ninth and tenth centuries. The Crusaders annexed it in 1203 and used it as a Roman Catholic church until 1261, when it was regained by the Greek Church. When, in 1453, it fell into the hands of the Turks, it was converted into a Mosque, and the mosaics were covered with whitewash. The minarets and other out-buildings were added during the period of Moslem dominion. In 1847 the Italian architect Fossati restored the structure as nearly as possible to its original form, and it remained for Mustapha Kemal, after converting it into a museum in 1934, to permit the work of completely uncovering the original mosaics, which work is still in progress.

Sancta Sophia is the largest and most magnificent of all the monuments of Byzantine architecture, and constitutes one of the crowning architectural achievements of man. It is roughly square in shape, having a central space of some 11,500 sq. ft., covered by one vast dome springing from arches 130 ft. from the ground and supported by two semi-domes of equal diameter, creating one uninterrupted oval space 214 ft. long by 107 ft. wide. The building is mainly constructed of brick. The interior walls are faced with marble, and the vaults, domes and pendentives are enriched with superb mosaics of coloured glass on a gold background.

THE ARCHITECTURAL BACKGROUND

The chart on the following pages is designed to indicate, in chronological order, the major changes in European architecture over a period of about 1200 years. All the buildings are drawn to the same scale so that one can see not only their characteristic plan shapes but also obtain some idea of the comparative bulk of the buildings selected. The choice of buildings has necessarily been limited, but as far as possible only those which are characteristic of the periods have been chosen.

The Byzantine or Eastern European architecture shows a continuous progression, while Western architecture, which grew directly out of the older Roman forms, and was subject to periodic influences from the East, developed a series of distinguishable styles each one more or less distinct from its predecessors. Byzantine architecture is characterised by the use of the dome on a square plan as the central and culminating feature of the building ; and Western architecture, by the development of the idea of the long nave vista which culminated in the Sanctuary at the eastern end. Byzantine architecture owes its origin to Eastern forms which were developed in Constantinople by Greek craftsmen. The first perfected building with a centralised dome over a square space was the church of Sancta Sophia, built by the Emperor Justinian in the sixth century. No other building equal in size or magnificence was ever attempted in the East. The structural developments that took place in the subsequent centuries were modest and unimportant. This perfect plan form having been achieved, churches were built throughout the Empire smaller in size, simpler in detail, but always maintaining that essential characteristic of an uninterrupted central space covered by a dome. Domes latterly were raised on high drums punctuated by narrow windows, a feature which was to be adopted in Western Europe in the Renaissance in the form of a colonnaded peristyle, as can be seen at S. Peter's, Rome, and S. Paul's, London. An additional characteristic of the later Byzantine was the multiplication of domes, as at S. Mark's, Venice, and many of the later churches of Greece, and which culminated in the fantastic clusters of bulbous forms which are typical of latter day Russian architecture. Domes are placed, not only over the central space, but on the arms of the cross or on the four corners which complete the cross in square plan.

The Byzantine plan form was particularly suited to the ritual of the Greek Orthodox Church, just as the long processional nave was suited to the Western or Latin-Catholic. It provided, in the East, the opportunity for the systematic arrangement of instructional mosaics or frescoes which covered the extensive internal wall surfaces. Byzantine culture spread far beyond the limits of the Empire. It is to be seen in the domed churches of Aquitaine, in the mosaiced interiors of many Roman basilicas, in Russia and Rumania, Sicily and Spain, and has persisted in South-Eastern Europe up to the present day.

DEVELOPMENT OF ARCHITECTURE

EASTERN

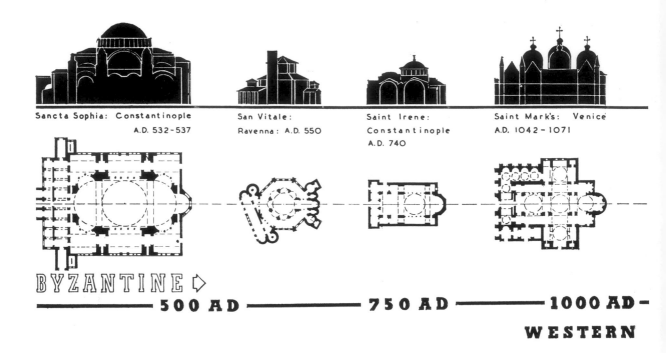

Sancta Sophia: Constantinople
A.D. 532-537

San Vitale:
Ravenna: A.D. 550

Saint Irene:
Constantinople
A.D. 740

Saint Mark's: Venice
A.D. 1042-1071

BYZANTINE ▷ ── 500 AD ── 750 AD ── 1000 AD ─

WESTERN

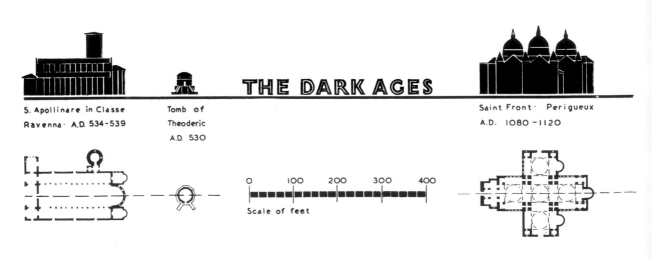

S. Apollinare in Classe
Ravenna· A.D. 534-539

Tomb of
Theoderic
A.D. 530

THE DARK AGES

Saint Front· Perigueux
A.D. 1080-1120

Scale of feet
0 100 200 300 400

EARLY
CHRISTIAN ARCHITECTURE WAS LIMITED TO N. ITALY. FROM THIS DEVELOPED ROMANESQUE AND

190

EUROPEAN

| Saint Luke Phocis, Greece: A.D. 1076 | S.Cataldo Palermo Sicily: A.D. 1130 | Holy Apostles Salonika Greece A.D. 1200 | Pantanassa Mistra Greece A.D. 1400 | Dochiariou Mount Athos Greece AD.1558 | Saint Basil Moscow A.D. 1555-1560 | Saint John Yaroslav Russia: A.D. 1671 |

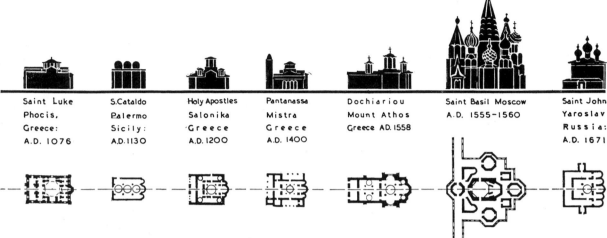

BYZANTINE ▷

─── 1250 AD ─── 1500 AD ───

EUROPEAN

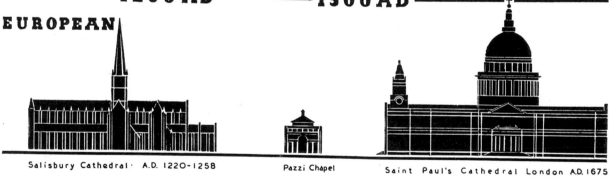

Salisbury Cathedral· A.D. 1220-1258

Pazzi Chapel Florence A.D. 1429

Saint Paul's Cathedral London A.D. 1675

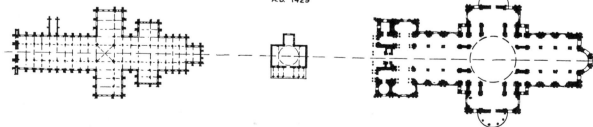

ULTIMATELY THE GOTHIC, AN INTELLECTUAL REVIVAL IN ITALY LED TO THE RENAISSANCE ▷

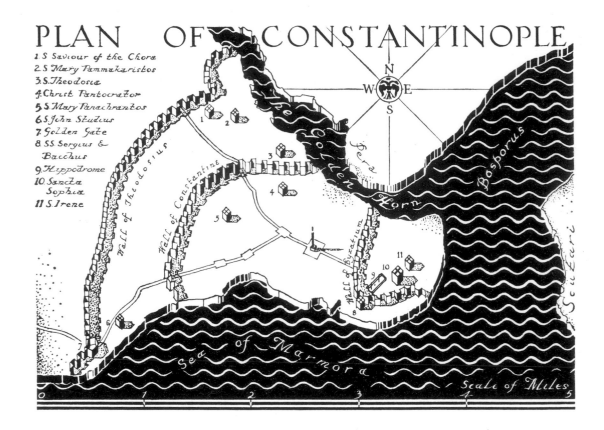

PLAN OF CONSTANTINOPLE

1. S. Saviour of the Chora
2. S. Mary Pammakaristos
3. S. Theodosia
4. Christ Pantocrator
5. S. Mary Panachrantos
6. S. John Studius
7. Golden Gate
8. SS. Sergius & Bacchus
9. Hippodrome
10. Sancta Sophia
11. S. Irene

SOME NOTES ON CONSTANTINOPLE

The Greek city of Byzantium, founded in 666 B.C. by Dorian Greeks, was chosen by Constantine the Great in A.D. 324 as " New Rome," and was later styled Constantinople to commemorate its founder. The choice was of great significance for strategic, commercial and cultural reasons. The city stood on a promontory at the junction of two important trade routes which linked Asia and Europe by land and sea, and the Golden Horn to the north provided a magnificent natural harbour. The new capital, by virtue of its central position, was able to command the eastern possessions of the Roman Empire while maintaining contact with the West.

Standing, like Rome, on seven hills, and bounded on two sides by the Bosporus and the Sea of Marmora, the city was an easy one to defend and to extend. The original walls bounding Byzantium on the west confined too small a city for the new capital of the Roman Empire, and Constantine completed a new wall further west on the 11th May, A.D. 330. In the fifth century the city reached its furthest limits, comprising an area of 4000 acres, when Theodosius erected his great wall still further west, which withstood the attacks of the Huns and remained inviolate until the Fourth Crusade in 1204. This wall stands to-day on the outskirts of the present city.

The new city was laid out on Roman lines and had an excellent water supply, carried in by aqueducts and stored in vast underground cisterns, which are still used. Constantine

192

chose a site in the south-east part of the old city for his imperial palace. To the west of the palace was built the Hippodrome, where the Roman games took place; Sancta Sophia stood north of the Hippodrome. These three great buildings shared between them most of the important historical events of the city.

Estimates of the population of Constantinople vary between 500,000 and 1,000,000 souls. It was by far the largest city in Europe and contained innumerable churches, of which only comparatively few remain. Those indicated on the map above are only the churches referred to in the text of this book.

THE GEOGRAPHICAL BACKGROUND

The map on the following two pages indicates, in a general way, the areas and places where the chief building developments took place in Europe from the time of Constantine up to the Renaissance in Europe.

It will be noticed that the physical limits of the Byzantine Empire do not always coincide with the extent of the Byzantine architectural influence. This is particularly noticeable in the Balkans north of the Danube and in Russia where Byzantine architecture developed long after the Empire had fallen to the Turks.

The Byzantine Empire reached its maximum extent in the reign of the Emperor Justinian (*circa* A.D. 560) when, according to calculations made by Edward Foord, it reached an area of just over a million square miles having a population of about 70 million persons. (About ten times the area of Great Britain and ten times the population of London.) Within 200 years the Empire had decreased by about half, having lost Syria, Mesopotamia and the North African coast as well as a large section of North Italy. After the Fourth Crusade the boundaries of the Empire were further curtailed; and when the final onslaught of the Ottoman Turks developed in the first quarter of the fifteenth century the Empire consisted of little more than a few square miles surrounding the capital.

THE GEOGRAPHICAL BACKGROUND

BYZANTINE ARCHITECTURE
A.D. 350..............

EARLY CHRISTIAN ARCHITECTURE
A.D. 300-900

ROMANESQUE ARCHITECTURE
A.D. 900-1200

GOTHIC ARCHITECTURE
A.D. 1200-1500

SLAVS

LIMIT OF CHARLEMAGNE'S EMPIRE 814 A.D.

Aix la Chapelle

GOTHIC INVASIONS

THE ALPS

THE BYZANTINE EMPIRE CIRCA

Périgueux

Venice

A.D. 493

Ravenna

A.D. 560

Rome

Naples

A.D. 750

M E D I T E R R A N E A N

Palermo

THE BOUNDARY OF THE BYZANTINE EMPIRE CIRCA A.D. 560.

SELECT LIST OF THE PRINCIPAL
BYZANTINE BUILDINGS

AIX LA CHAPELLE :
Cathedral

ANI :
Cathedral
Chapel of S. Gregory

ATHENS :
Kapnikarea
Metropole
S. Theodore

ATHOS :
Dochiariou
Lavra
Simopetra

CONSTANTINOPLE :
S. Irene
S. Saviour in the Chora
S. Theodore
SS. Sergius & Bacchus
Sancta Sophia
Walls

JERUSALEM :
Church of the Holy Sepulchre

KIEV :
S. Saviour
S. Sophia

METEORA :
S. Stephanos
S. Barlaam

MISTRA :
Covent of Pantanassa
Peribleptos

MOSCOW :
The Kremlin
S. Basil

NAPLES :
Baptistery of Sotor

NOVGOROD :
Nereditsi
S. Sophia
SS. Boris & Gleb

PALERMO :
Cappella Palatina
La Cubola
Monreale Cathedral
S. Cataldo

PERIGUEUX :
S. Front

RAVENNA :
The Orthodox Baptistery
S. Apollinare in Classe
S. Apollinare Nuovo
S. Vitale
Tomb of Galla Placidia

RUTHWELL :
Stone Cross

SALONIKA :
Holy Apostles
S. Dometrius
S. George
S. Sophia

SUCAVITA :
Monastery

TREBIZOND :
The Chrysokephalos
S. Sophia

VENICE :
S. Marks

Bibliography

This bibliography does not pretend to be exhaustive : it includes those books which were consulted and which seemed to me useful.

GENERAL HISTORY

The Cambridge Mediæval History, Vols. I and IV.   Cambridge, 1923.

BAYNES, N.   *The Byzantine Empire*.   London, 1925.

BURY, J. B.   *History of the Eastern Roman Empire* (395-565).   London, 1889.

—— *History of the Later Roman Empire* (802-867).   London, 1912.

BYRON, R.   *The Byzantine Achievement*.   London, 1929.

DINER, H.   *Emperors, Angels and Eunuchs*.   London, 1938.

FINLEY, G.   *History of the Byzantine Empire*.   London, 1906.

FOORD, E.   *The Byzantine Empire*.   London, 1911.

JORGA, N.   *The Byzantine Empire*.   London, 1907.

OMAN, C. W. C.   *The Byzantine Empire*.   London, 1892.

ROBERTSON, J. M.   *A Short History of Christianity*.   London, 1908.

VILLEHARDOUIN and DE JOINVILLE.   *Memoirs of the Crusades*.   London, 1908.

ART AND ARCHITECTURE

BROWNE, E. A.   *Byzantine Architecture*.   London, 1912.

BYRON, R. and RICE, T.   *The Birth of Western Painting*.   London, 1930.

CHOISY, A.   *L'Art de bâtir chez le Byzantins*.   Paris, 1883.

DALTON, O. M.   *Byzantine Art and Archæology*.   Oxford, 1911.

—— *Guide to Early Christian and Byzantine Antiquities in the British Museum*.   London, 1921.

—— *East Christian Art*.   Oxford, 1925.

DIEHL, C.   *Manuel D'Art Byzantin*.   Paris, 1925.

HAMILTON, J. A.   *Byzantine Architecture and Decoration*.   London, 1934.

JACKSON, T. G.   *Byzantine and Romanesque Architecture*.   Cambridge, 1913.

LETHABY, W. R.   *Mediæval Art*.   London, 1912.

LOWRIE, W.   *Christian Art and Archæology*.   New York, 1901.

PEIRCE, H. and TYLER, R.   *Byzantine Art*.   London, 1926.

RICE, T.   *Byzantine Art*.   Oxford, 1935.

RIVOIRA, G. T.   *Lombardic Architecture*.   London, 1910.

STRZYGOWSKI, J.   *Origin of Christian Church Art*.   Oxford, 1923.

—— *Early Church Art in Northern Europe*.   London, 1928.

CONSTANTINOPLE

LETHABY, W. R. and SWAINSON, H.   *The Church of Sancta Sophia, Constantinople.   A Study of Byzantine Building*.   London, 1894.

VAN MILLINGEN, A.   *Byzantine Constantinople* (the walls of the city).   London, 1899.

—— *Constantinople*.   London, 1906.

—— *Byzantine Churches in Constantinople*.   London, 1912.

YOUNG, G.   *Constantinople*, London, 1926.

GREECE

BREWSTER, R. *The 6000 Beards of Athos.* London, 1935.

BYRON, R. *The Station.* London, 1928.

CHOUKAS, M. *Black Angels of Athos.* London, 1935.

CURSON, R. *Visits to Monasteries in the Levant.* London, 1916.

DAWKINS, R. M. *The Monks of Athos.* London, 1936.

HAMILTON, J. A. *The Church of Kaisariani in Attica and its Frescoes.* Aberdeen, 1916.

HASLUCK, F. W. *Athos and its Monasteries.* London, 1924.

RILEY, A. *Athos, or The Mountain of the Monks.* London, 1887.

SCHULTZ, R. W. and BARNSLEY, S. H. *The Monastery of Saint Luke of Stiris in Phocis.*
London, 1901.

ITALY

HAMILTON, J. A. *Churches in Palermo.* London, 1929.

HUTTON, E. *Ravenna.* London, 1913.

JACKSON, F. H. *Sicily.* New York, 1925.

—— *The Shores of the Adriatic. The Italian Side.* London, 1906.

RICCI, C. *Ravenna.* Bergamo, 1903.

RUSKIN, J. *Byzantine Churches in Venice.* (From the Stones of Venice.) London, 1908.

WAERN, C. *Mediæval Sicily.* London, 1910.

WESTERN EUROPE

BROWN, G. BALDWIN. *The Ruthwell and Bewcastle Crosses.* 1921.

CASSON, S. *Greece and Britain.* London, 1943.

CLAPHAM, A. W. *Romanesque Architecture in Western Europe.* Oxford, 1936.

—— *English Romanesque Architecture before the Conquest.* Oxford, 1930.

DINWIDDIE, J. L. *The Ruthwell Cross.* Dumfries, 1927.

GARDNER, A. *Mediæval Sculpture in France.* London, 1931.

198

Index

(Illustrations shown in heavy type)

Agioi Saranta, Peloponnesus, Church, 127, **129**, 131
Agios Loukas, Monastery of, 30, **31**, 32, 33
Agios Sotiros, Attica, Church, 36, **41**, **42**, 43
Allivi, Church, 133, **136**
Aquitaine, 23, 29, 123
Asomatoi, Church, 44
Asteri, Attica, Monastery, 27
Athanasius, 83
Athens, 18-29, 32, 33, 34, 43, 44, **45**, 137
  Acropolis, 18
  Asomatoi, Church, 44
  Byzantine Museum, 43, 44, 69
  Holy Apostles, Church, 44
  Kapnikarea, Church, 20, **21**
  Metropolitan Cathedral, 23
  Parthenon, 18
  S. Nicodemus, Church, 24, **25**, 26, 32
  S. Theodore, Church, 24
  Small Cathedral (Metropole), **22**, 23, 24
Athos, Mount, 55-93 (see also Monasteries)
  Government of, 59, 64, 66
Attica, 27, 29, 30

Baptistry, Ravenna, 164, **165**, 166
Baroque Architecture, 11
Basil I, 23
Basil II, 18
Belisarius, 166
Blomfield, Sir Reginald, 12
Brindisi, 138, 139
Byron, Lord, 18
Byron, Robert, 106
Byzantine Art and Architecture :
  Dome Construction, 16, 17, 19
  Frescoes, 18, 24, 29, 35, 36, 52, 62, **63**, **90**, **91**, 120,
    122, 123, 127, **128**
  Ikonastasis, 20, 44, 62, 98
  Ikons, *Frontispiece*, 43, 44, 57, 64, 66, 69, 76,
    77, **78**
  Ikons, Mosaic, 69
  Interiors, **88**, **91**, **100**, **151**, **152**, **167**, **170**, **171**
  Mosaics, Floor, 33, 102
    Wall, 20, 32, 33, 49, 51, 69, 102, 105, 106, 146,
    147, **148**, 150, **151**, **152**, 158, **159**, **165**, **167**,
    170, **171**, **173**, 174, **175**, **177**
  Narthex, 27, 64

Byzantine Art and Architecture, *cont.* :
  Phiale, 70, 74, 76, 85, **87**
  Sculpture, 43, 49, 50, 51, 120, **121**, **169**, 178, **179**,
    180, **181**, **182**, 183
  Squinch, 16, **17**, 24, 26, **151**
  Structure, 19, 20, 24, 26, 32, 35, 44, 49, 51, 79, 83,
    97, 98
Byzantine Museum, Athens, 43, 44, 69
Byzantium, see Constantinople

Cantaguzene, Emperor, 35
Capella Palatina, Palermo, 150, **151**
Castelvetrano :
    SS. Trinita di Delia, 153, **154**
Catacombs of S. Callistus, Rome, 160
Cefalu, Cathedral, 156, 157
Cenobian Government of Athos, 64, 66
Chartres Cathedral, 178, 180, **181**, **182**
Christ Pantocrator, Constantinople, Church of, 111,
  113
Christ, physiognomy of, **78**, 105, 164
Churches (see also Monasteries)
  Agia Saranda, Peloponnesus, 127, **129**, 131
  Agios Sotiros, Attica, 36, **41**, **42**, 43
  Allivi, 133, **136**
  Asomatoi, Athens, 44
  Asteri, 27
  Capella Palatina, Palermo, 150, **151**
  Chartres Cathedral, 178, 180, **181**, **182**
  Christ Pantocrator, Constantinople, 111, **113**
  Crissafa, Peloponnesus, 126, 127, **128**
  Daphni, near Athens, 33
  Holy Apostles, Athens, 44
  Holy Apostles, Salonika, **48**, 52, **53**, **54**
  Kaisariani, Attica, 27, **28**, 29
  Kapnikarea, Athens, 20, **21**
  Karlskirche, Vienna, 11, 12
  Metropole, see Small Cathedral, Athens
  Monreale, Cathedral, 150, **152**, 153
  Omorphi Ecclesia, Attica, **34**, 43
  Pantanassa, Mistra, 117, 120, **122**, 123, **124**
  Peribleptos, Mistra, 123, **125**, 126
  Prodromus, Athos, 76
  Protaton, Athos, 57
  S. Apollinare in Classe, **170**, 172
  S. Apollinare Nuovo, Ravenna, 166, **167**, 168

Churches (see also Monasteries), *cont.*
  S. Baarlam, Meteora, 35, **40**
  S. Cataldo, Palermo, **149**
  S. Demetrius, Mistra, 117, 118, **119**, 120, **121, 130**
  S. Demetrius, Salonika, 49, 50, 51, 52, 105
  S. George, Salonika, 51
  S. Giovanni degli Eremeti, Palermo, 142, **143, 144**
  S. John of the Studion, Constantinople, 101, 102
  S. Luke, Stiris, **31,** 32, 33
  S. Maria dell' Ammiraglio, Church, 146, **147, 148, 151**
  S. Mark, Rossano, 140, **141**
  S. Mark, Venice, 101, 123, 172, 174, **175, 176, 177**
  S. Mary Pammakaristos, Constantinople, **112**
  S. Nicholas, Meteora, **37**
  S. Nicholas, Monamvasia, 133, **134, 135**
  S. Nicodemus, Athens, 24, **25,** 26, 32
  S. Peter, Rome, 160, 161
  S. Restituta, Naples, Basilica of, 158, **159**
  S. Saviour, Constantinople (Karieh Djami), 102, **103, 104,** 105, 106
  S. Sophia, Constantinople, see Sancta Sophia
  S. Sophia, Monamvasia, 131, **132**
  S. Sophia, Salonika, 47, 49
  S. Stephen, Meteora, 35
  S. Theodore, Athens, 24
  S. Theodosia, Constantinople (Gul Djami), 106 **107,** 108
  S. Vitale, Ravenna, **171,** 172
  SS. Nicola and Cataldo, Lecce, 139
  SS. Trinita di Delia, Castelvetrano, 153, **154**
  Sancta Sophia, Constantinople, 32, 96, 97, **97,** 98, **99, 100,** 101, 114
  Small Cathedral, Athens, **22,** 23, 24
Codex Rossanensis, 140
Constantine (the Great), 14, 23, 94, 160
Constantine XI, 116, 118
Constantinople, 14, 23, 32, 94-116, 144
  Christ Pantocrator, Church of, 111, **113**
  Cisterns, 110, 111
  Mosque of Sultan Ahmet, 114, **115**
  S. John of the Studion, 101, 102
  S. Mary Pammakaristos, **112**
  S. Saviour (Karieh Djami), Church, 102, **103, 104,** 105, 106
  S. Theodosia (Gul Djami), Church, 106 **107,** 108
  Sancta Sophia, Church of, 32, 96, **97,** 97, 98, **99, 100,** 101, 114
  Tekfour Serai, 109, 144
Crissafa, Peloponnesus, Church at, 126, 127, **128**
Cross, Holy, 33, 83, 85
Crusades, 95, 101, 116, 178
Curzon, Robert, 36

D'Annunzio, Gabriele, 13
Daou-Mendeli, Monastery of, 44

Daphni, Athos, 55, 57, 93
Daphni, near Athens, 33
Dawkins, R. M., 70
Diocletian, 14, 15, 23, 94
Dionysiou, Athos, Monastery, 89, **92,** 93
Dionysius, 89
Dochiariou, Athos, Monastery, 74, **75,** 76, 79

Edict of Milan, 94
Eirene, Empress, 111
Elgin, Lord, 18
El Greco, 29

Frescoes, 18, 24, 29, 35, 36, 52, 62, **63, 90, 91,** 120, **122,** 123, 127, **128**

Galla Placidia, Mausoleum of, Ravenna, 163, 164
Government of Athos, 64, 66
Gregory of Nin, Bishop, 14
Gul Djami, Constantinople, see S. Theodosia, under Churches

Haloes, 168
Henry IV of England, 133
Holy Apostles, Athens, Church of the, 44
Holy Apostles, Salonika, Church of the, **48,** 52, **53, 54**
Holy Cross, 33, 83, 85
Hymettos, Mount :
  Asteri, Church, 27
  Kaisariani, Church, 27, **28,** 29

Idiorythmic Government of Athos, 64, 66
Ikonastasis, 20, 44, 62, 98
Ikons, *Frontispiece,* 43, 44, 57, 64, 66, 69, 76, **77, 78**
Ikons, mosaic, 69
Ivan III of Russia, 118
Iveron, Athos, Monastery, **58,** 69, 70, 71

Justinian, 166, 168, 172, **173**

Kaisariani, Attica, Church, 27, **28,** 29
Kalabaka, 35
Kapnikarea, Athens, Church, 20, **21**
Karieh Djami, Constantinople, see S. Saviour, under Churches
Karlskirche, Vienna, 11, 12
Karyes, Athos, 57, **58**
  Church of the Protaton, 57

Kemal, Mustapha, 108, 114
Kerasia, Athos, 85, 89

Lavra, Great, Athos, Monastery, 83, **84,** 85, **87**
Lecce, S. Italy :
    SS. Nicola and Cataldo, 139

Manuel II, 133
Mausoleum :
    of Diocletian, Spalat, 15, 17
    of Galla Placidia, Ravenna, 163, 164
    of Theodoric, Ravenna, 166
Maximianus, Chair of, Ravenna, **169,** 172
Mestrovic, Ivan, 14, 15
Meteora, **34,** 35, 36, **37, 39, 40**
Metropole, Athens, see Small Cathedral, under Churches
Metropolitan Cathedral, Athens, 23
Michael III, 23
Michael VIII (Paleologus), 116
Mistra, 106, 116-126
    Pantanassa, Convent of, 117, 120, **122,** 123, **124**
    Peribleptos, Church, 123, **125,** 126
    S. Demetrius, Church, 117, 118, **119,** 120, **121, 130**
Mithra, 95
Mohammedans, 23, 52, 59, 96, 98, 108, 111, 116
Monamvasia, **130,** 131, **132,** 133, **134, 135**
    S. Nicholas, Church, 133, **134, 135**
    S. Sophia, Church, 131, **132**
Monasteries :
    Agias Loukas, 30, **31,** 32, 33
    Asteri, Attica, 27
    Daou-Mendeli, 44
    Dionysiou, Athos, 89, **92,** 93
    Dochiariou, Athos, 74, **75,** 76, 79
    Iveron, Athos, **58,** 69, 70, 71
    Lavra, Great, Athos, 83, **84,** 85, **87**
    Meteora, **34,** 35, 36, **37, 39, 40**
    Pantanassa, Mistra (Convent), 117, 120, **122,** 123, **124**
    Pantocrator, Athos, 64, 66
    Russico, Athos, 71, **72,** 73
    Simopetra, Athos, 79, **80, 81, 82,** 83
    Stavronikita, Athos, 66, 69
    Vatopedi, Athos, 59, **60, 61,** 62, 64
Monreale, Sicily, Cathedral, 150, **152,** 153
Mosaics, 20, 32, 33, 49, 51, 69, 102, 105, 106, 146, **147, 148,** 150, **151, 152,** 158, **159, 165, 167, 170, 171, 173,** 174, **175, 177**
Mosaic ikons, 69
Moscow :
    S. Basil, Church, 96, 118
Mosque of Sultan Ahmet, Constantinople, 114, **115**
Mount Athos, 55-93

Naples :
    S. Restituta, Basilica of, 158, **159**
Nicea, 116
    Council of, 166
Nicephorus II, Phocas, 83

Omorphi Ecclesia, Attica, **34,** 43

Palace :
    of Diocletian, Spalato, 14
    of Tekfour Serai, Constantinople, 109, 144
Palermo, 140-151
    Capella Palatina, 150, **151**
    Piccolo Cubola, 144, **145,** 146
    S. Cataldo, **149**
    S. Giovanni degli Eremeti, Church, 142, **143,** 144
    S. Maria dell' Ammiraglio, Palermo, 146, **147, 148, 151**
Pantanassa, Mistra, Convent of the, 117, 120, **122,** 123, **124**
Pantocrator, Athos, Church, 64, 66
Peribleptos, Mistra, Church, 123, **125,** 126
Perigueux, 101
Phiale, 70, 74, 76, 85, **87**
Piccola Cubola, Palermo, 144, **145,** 146
Prodromus, Athos, Church, 76
Protaton, Athos, Church of the, 57

Rasputin, 73
Ravenna, 163-173
    Baptistry, 164, **165,** 166
    Chair of Maximianus, **169,** 172
    Mausoleum of Galla Placidia, 163, 164
    S. Apollinare in Classe, near Ravenna, Church, **170,** 172
    S. Apollinare Nuovo, Church, 166, **167,** 168
    S. Vitale, Church, **171,** 172
Rivoira, G. T., 47
Rome, 94, 95, 158, 160-162
    Catacombs of S. Callistus, 160
    S. Peter, 160, 161
Rossano, 139, 140, **141**
    S. Mark, Church, 140, **141**
    Codex Rossanensis, 140
Ruskin, John, 43, 105, 178
Russia, 71, 73, 95, 118
Russico, Athos, Monastery, 71, **72,** 73
Ruthwell, Scotland, 180, 183

Salonika, 47-54, 105
    Holy Apostles, Church, **48,** 52, **53, 54**
    S. Demetrius, Church, 49-52, 105
    S. George, Church, 51
    S. Sophia, Church, 47, 49

Scutari, 95
Simopetra, Athos, Monastery, 79, **80, 81, 82,** 83
Spalato, 14, 15
   Palace of Diocletian, 14
   Mausoleum of Diocletian, 14-17
Stavronikita, Athos, Monastery, 66, 69
Susak, 13

Tekfour Serai, Constantinople, 109, 144
Theodora, Empress, 172
Theodoric (the Austrogoth) :
   Baptistry of, Ravenna, 164, **165,** 166
   Mausoleum of, Ravenna, 166
Torcello, 178, **179**

Treaty of Lausanne, 59
Trebizond, 23, 116
Tunis, 155, 156
Turks, see Mohammedans

Vatopedi, Athos, Monastery, 59, **60, 61,** 62, 64
Venice, 101, 123, 172, 174-178
   S. Mark, 101, 123, 172, 174, **175, 176, 177**
Vienna, 11-13
   Karlskirche, 11, 12
Villehardouin, Geoffrey, 101, 116, 123, 133
Von Erlach, Fischer, 11, 12

Wheler, Sir George, 32

GEORGE ALLEN & UNWIN LTD
London: 40 Museum Street, W.C.1

Auckland: 24 Wyndham Street
Bombay: 15 Graham Road, Ballard Estate, Bombay 1
Calcutta: 17 Chittaranjan Avenue, Calcutta 13
Cape Town: 109 Long Street
Karachi: Metherson's Estate, Wood Street, Karachi 2
New Delhi: 13-14 Ajmeri Gate Extension, New Delhi 1
São Paulo: Avenida 9 de Julho 1138-Ap. 51
Sydney, N.S.W.: Bradbury House, 55 York Street
Toronto: 91 Wellington Street West

Serbian Legacy

CECIL STEWART

That Serbia made any contribution at all to the sum of architectural history will come as a surprise to those whose knowledge is limited to the standard text-books. That Serbia made a contribution to art has only been generally recognised since 1953, when a remarkable collection of reproductions of Yugoslav frescos was exhibited in various countries in the West. The architecture which enshrines these frescos has been largely unrecognised and unrecorded. Now, for the first time in English, this important gap has been filled, and the splendour of the Serbian medieval legacy is apparent.

For three hundred years Serbia was probably more productive of great art and architecture than any other country in the Byzantine world. The inspiration was Byzantine, but, as the author shows, special regional characteristics were developed. The book, which is very fully illustrated by magnificent photographs and by detailed drawings, also makes reference to the Muslim developments and to the most curious Bogomil sect, with its mysterious carved monuments. It should enthral the student of architecture, the visitor to Yugoslavia and the stay-at-home traveller.

Cr. 4to.   About 42s. net

Guide to Western Architecture

JOHN GLOAG

" . . . . One of the virtues of this survey, which keeps a firm grasp on detail yet marshals the trends and currents of the art, is that Mr. Gloag's sympathies are alert and eclectic.

BOOKS OF THE MONTH

" . . . . well planned, always readable and profusely illustrated. Unlike similar guides, it pays proper attention to Greece and Rome without ignoring the influence of Byzantium and Islam on Western architecture. Nor does it slur over the architecture of Germany, Spain and the Low Countries . . . . "

TIMES EDUCATIONAL SUPPLEMENT

Cr. 4to.   63s. net

GEORGE ALLEN & UNWIN LTD